JIM CRAWFORD

Lessons in Courage

For Emily and Jeff

First published February 2023

Copyright *Kevin Guthrie*

ISBN 978-1-7391249-2-2

Author *Kevin Guthrie*
Designer *Charles Goddard*
Front cover
Main image *Author's collection*
Bottom left and centre *Christopher Mann*
Bottom right *Tim Marshall*
Rear cover *Alan Cox*

Printer *The Manson Group Ltd*
Publisher *Performance Publishing Ltd*
Grantham, Lincolnshire

Contents

Acknowledgements   *6*

Foreword - Bob Fernley   *8*

Introduction   *10*

Chapter One   Fife Born, Lancashire Bred   *14*

Chapter Two   A Helping Hand   *20*

Chapter Three   Frantic Atlantic   *24*

Chapter Four   Brief Encounters of the F1 Kind   *34*

Chapter Five   What Now, Jim?   *42*

Chapter Six   Back on Track   *48*

Chapter Seven   European Swansong   *56*

Chapter Eight   Transatlantic Traveller   *64*

Chapter Nine   The Start of a Love Affair   *74*

Chapter Ten   Turn One   *84*

Chapter Eleven   A Lesson in Courage   *88*

Chapter Twelve   Getting His Wings and Other Adventures   *94*

Chapter Thirteen   Back with Bernstein   *102*

Chapter Fourteen   233.433   *106*

Chapter Fifteen   Last Time Out   *114*

Chapter Sixteen   Time Running Out   *120*

Index   *128*

Bibliography   *132*

About the Author   *133*

Acknowledgements

esearching Jim's story has brought me into contact with a vast and eclectic array of people from all over the globe. The renowned motorsport photographer, David Hutson, was the person responsible for talking me into the project in the first instance. After a frustrating start, during which time I struggled to find relatives and close friends of Jim, a letter to *The Bolton News* opened a veritable floodgate of contributors. Jim's great friend, Rob Moores, very kindly arranged a meeting in 2010 at a public house in Belmont, the village with the sailing club where Jim was a member. At that meeting I first made the acquaintance of Jim's sister, Jean Boardman. Jean, along with her cousin, Jeff Shuttleworth, have proved invaluable. Aside from their own memories of growing up with Jim I was privileged to be given access to family albums. Many of the photos from these are reproduced in the following pages for the first time. Also at that initial meeting was Sue Deakin, Jim's former long-term girlfriend, who was only too happy to share her memories and photographs. Paddy Atkinson provided insight into another great love of Jim's life, sailing. I also received a memorable lift back to my hotel from Jim's former rally co-driver, 'Fess' Parker.

Having never written a book before, I admit to having been somewhat nervous about calling Bob Fernley. Bob was a principal of the Force India Formula One team at the time, and I wasn't sure how much he would appreciate a stranger calling, during a busy Formula One season, to discuss a driver he had been involved with more than quarter of a century earlier. Of course, anyone who knows Bob will know I should have harboured no such reservations. He started by revealing that Jim was his favourite driver to have worked with, and he has worked with many great talents. Over many email exchanges, Bob was able to fill in some important gaps in Jim's racing history, particularly regarding his forays into India. I am also indebted to Bob for agreeing to write the foreword to this book about his old friend. I can think of nobody better to introduce the story of Jim's life.

One of the more trying periods during my research concerned Jim's time in Switzerland, working for Toyota. After a few dead-ends a tip-off led me to Mike Peers, who invited me down to his holiday home in the Lake District. Mike had accompanied Jim to Switzerland, and was a crucial source of information. He also loaned me personal photo albums of his time with Jim. Jim's Formula Atlantic teammate, Stephen Choularton, was another important person in the story. Having eventually tracked him down in Australia, Stephen was delighted to recall those heady days of the 1970s, when he played a pivotal role in Jim's early racing career.

Jim was synonymous with Chevron. Neil Bailey, Neil Edwards, Kevin Hodgkinson and Dave Taylor all worked with Jim and were happy to share their memories. At Dave's house I also had the chance to speak to well- known commentator Richard Sproston, a great friend and fan of Jim, who sadly passed away before this book was published.

Much of Jim's life was spent in the US, and he developed a love affair with the Indianapolis 500. Roman Kuzma, Keith Leighton and Kenny Bernstein all shared extensive memories of their time running Jim at the Brickyard. Rivals were also happy to chat about a man they had fond memories of. Derck Daly, Bobby Rahal and Tom Sneva all raced with Jim, and Willy T Ribbs provided me with an interview I shall long remember. Team owner Ron Hemelgarn was another admirer of Jim's character, and also helped with his recuperation following the catastrophic accident Jim suffered at Indianapolis in 1987.

Jim led a somewhat nomadic life for several years in the States, which led me to track down such fascinating people as Canadian country music star Brian Good and Can Am rival John Graham. I spoke to drivers who raced against Jim from all periods of his career. Thanks to Bernard Devaney, Gordon Gonsalves, Kim Mather, Jacques Villeneuve and Ted Wentz for their recollections. Also, to Jim's teammates I interviewed: Joe Castellano, Roberto Guerrero and Whitney Ganz.

Jim had many friends in the racing world, and stories for this book have not been in short supply. Among those who have shared some memorable tales are Bruce Ashmore, Tino Belli, Tommy Byrne, Keith Humphreys, Richard Jones, Chris Kellett, Marcus Pye and Mark Scott. A special thanks goes to Adam Wilkins, Charles Goddard and Sarah Scrimshaw at Performance Publishing. I have had the pleasure of working with Adam and Sarah before, on a book about Tom Pryce, which I wrote along with my great friend, Darren Banks. It was Darren who first introduced me to Adam, and I couldn't have asked for a better publisher. Adam has given unknown writers a chance in the past few years, and his faith has certainly been repaid by them. I only hope this book continues to uphold the high standards set by previous efforts. Darren penned Performance Publishing's first motorsport book in 2017, a wonderful biography of Stephen South. It was a finalist in the RAC Motoring Book of the Year, a competition won by another book produced by Adam in 2020. This was my friend Richard Jenkins' bio of Ritchie Ginther, which also landed the prestigious Montagu of Beaulieu Trophy. Both Darren and Richard have been very supportive of my own book, as has multi-award-winning journalist and author, Ian Wagstaff. In his excellent 2010 book, *The British at Indianapolis*, Ian dedicated a whole chapter to Jim. As an unknown author I have been somewhat humbled by Ian's kindness to me. In addition to giving me permission to lift any quotes I wished to use from his book, he also went to the trouble of digging out interviews he had recorded when researching Jim's career at Indianapolis himself.

On a personal level, I would like to thank my family for their support: Tracy, Amelia and Daniel. My mum and dad, for encouraging my early interest in the sport I have come to love. My friend and business partner, Laura Hodge, for tolerating my racing talk and realising I am a lost cause! Finally, to Lorraine Scouller, a dear friend of almost 30 years, for always showing interest in my projects, and giving her honest and constructive opinion on any material I have asked her to look over.

There have been many other people who have contributed memories and information for the book, and they are listed below. I can only apologise if I have omitted anyone. It is completely unintentional, and I am grateful to each and every person who has helped to tell Jim's story. Many thanks to the photographers, both amateur and professional, who have contributed images to the book. In a very small handful of cases, despite my best efforts, I have been unable to ascertain who captured certain images. If you recognise any belonging to yourself please get in touch so they can be suitably credited in any future editions.

Bob Abdellah, Mike Allen, Jay Alley, Susan Arnold, Tim Arnold, Bruce Ashmore, Tom Ashton, Paddy Atkinson, Neil Bailey, Jeremy Banks, Tino Belli, Hector Luis Bergandi, Kenny Bernstein, Jean Boardman, Alejandro de Brito, Felicity Brown, Ed Brunette, Tommy Byrne, Joe Castellano, Ian Catt, David Chapman, Stephen Choularton, Ronnie Condell, Alan Cooper, Alan Cox, Miranda Crompton, Rod Crompton, Derek Daly, Donald Davidson, Stuart Dent, Bernard Devaney, Janet Donnison, Neil Edwards, Dudley Evans, Bob Fernley, Andrew Fraser, David Free, Whitney Ganz, Graham Gauld, Charles Goddard, Gordon Gonsalves, Brian Good, John Graham, Roberto Guerrero, Henning Hagenbauer, John Hamer, Norman Hayes, Kevin Hodgkinson, Phil Hosker, Keith Humphreys, Carl Hungness, David Allen Hutson, George Jones, Richard Jones, Steve Jones, Chris Kellett, Rick Knoechel, Roman Kuzma, Rod Lee, Keith Leighton, Mark Lodge, Tim Marshall, Kim Mather, Pietro Meller, Robert Moores, Rob Neuzel, Iain Nicholson, Kurt Oblinger, Jackie Oliver, Dr Stephen Olvey, 'Fess' Parker, Derek Patai, Mike Peers, Marcus Pye, Bobby Rahal, Willy T Ribbs, Jim Robinson, Lawrence Rose, George Roux, Mary Rudkin, Mark Scott, Sarah Scrimshaw, Sue Shephard, Jeff Shuttleworth, Joe Skibinski, Julian Smith, Michael Smith, Phil Smithies, Tom Sneva, Richard Sproston, Simon Stiel, Anton Sukup, Dave Taylor, Geraldine Taylor, Peter Viccary, Jacques Villeneuve, Ian Wagstaff, Chris Walker, Ted Wentz, Geoff Werran and Adam Wilkins.

Foreword

I first met Jim in September of 1980 at a cold, wet and blustery Oulton Park racetrack. Against all odds, Jim won the feature Aurora race, driving a modified Formula Atlantic Chevron to beat an array of Formula One and Formula Two cars. While it could be argued the weather conditions favoured the lighter and nimbler Atlantic car, it was Jim's talent that shone through that day. Somehow, he tamed the appalling conditions to pull off the surprise win of the season. Fellow competitors, who were driving much quicker cars, were left in awe of how he overcame the weather and made the victory look so easy.

While this was my introduction to Jim's formidable driving skills, I also gained insight into another side of this impressive young lad from Bolton. Not only could he drive the wheels off anything you put under him, but he also demonstrated an unusual

Bob and Jim enjoyed some wonderful years together.
David Allen Hutson

humility in victory. He simply credited his win to the conditions suiting his car.

By 1982 we had developed a close working relationship with the Ensign Formula One Team and decided to enter the 1982 British Formula One Championship. There was no doubt in my mind that Jim was the man I wanted to drive the car. Over the year, my relationship with Jim grew stronger as we learned to trust each other in our respective roles. Jim won the British F1 Championship that year, but the biggest challenge was yet to come. We had decided to enter the Canadian American race series with a prototype Ensign Can Am car and embarked on what would be the start of an incredible racing partnership.

From race one in 1982, our North American adventure was successful. Jim finished runner up in his first Can Am event at Quebec's Trois-Rivières

Jim wasn't just another driver. He was a close friend. **Sue Deakin**

and, flushed with this early success, the real campaign began. One of our competitors described my guys as resembling the crew from a pirate ship and, with Jim steering the ship, we plundered our way across the length and breadth of the US and Canada, living what could only be described as a rock 'n' roll lifestyle. I had total belief that, if I could provide the equipment and car, Jim would deliver the results, which he did time and time again. We even expanded our racing schedule to include a winter series in India, where Jim became the first driver in Indian motor racing history to secure wins in the Madras GP three years in succession.

The partnership strengthened as we lived in each other's pockets for the next few years and shared many, many adventures. Without Jim, my career would not have received the boost I needed to get noticed in the world of motor racing, and for this I am eternally indebted.

> "Not only could he drive the wheels off anything you put under him, but he also demonstrated an unusual humility in victory"

The life of a professional racing driver is shaped not only by victories, but also by mistakes, mechanical failures and injuries. Sadly, Jim's final years were impacted by continual pain from a life-changing accident at the Brickyard in Indianapolis. While he was able to continue racing, his injuries profoundly altered his quality of life at a fundamental level.

Jim was unique. It is true he could be very demanding from a racing point of view, and annoyingly frustrating when it came to negotiating his financial package, when his Scottish genes came to the fore. As I look back on our years together, I appreciate that he was not only a naturally gifted driver, he was also a most humble, witty and loyal friend. For me, this will be his enduring legacy and lasting memory.

BOB FERNLEY

Introduction

Some days will stay a thousand years,
Some pass like the flash of a spark
East of Eden, Big Country

Sunday, May 29th, 1988: Indianapolis Motor Speedway, Indiana. Rick Mears has just joined an elite club, by winning his third Indianapolis 500, and thousands converge on Victory Circle to bask in his glory. Some distance away, in pit lane, another driver is attracting considerable attention. Jim Crawford brought his 1987 Buick-powered Lola home in sixth place yet, by the reaction of the spectators, you could be forgiven for thinking he was the victor. As Jim slowly and carefully emerges from the car thousands erupt in applause, and hollers of appreciation reverberate in the warm afternoon air. Jim himself would later reflect on the moment. "I was very surprised, but I love it. I lead a quiet life, and it's great. But they can do it any time they like."

The walking canes were the giveaway. The adoration had become a regular occurrence throughout that Month of

May, as fans seated in the bleachers behind Jim's pit box sympathised with his struggles and marvelled at the resolve required for him to even be there, let alone be competitive. Buick engineer Mark Scott witnessed it first-hand. "He would flash that big grin of his, and they truly thought they knew him, and were part of his comeback."

The comeback had started just over a year ago, as Jim lay in Methodist Hospital self-administering morphine as quickly as the machine would permit. His 1987 Indianapolis campaign had ended abruptly against the Turn One wall on May 9th, in a brutal front-end impact which left Jim trapped in his March-Buick with agonising lower leg injuries. The track's rescue personnel, as ever, were with their casualty within seconds. A necessarily slow extraction followed, before Jim was rushed to the Lifeline helicopter standing by.

The initial prognosis was grim, and amputation seemed

This photo was taken at Indianapolis in 1989, a year after Jim's remarkable comeback. He still required a cane to walk. Jim's injuries would affect him for the rest of his life. **Author's Collection**

a very real possibility. Famed surgeon Terry Trammell, an expert in treating lower leg injuries from racing accidents, would later recall, "His injuries were almost irreparable. IIis first round of surgery was about limb saving." Jim underwent multiple surgeries over the coming months. Supposedly confined to a wheelchair for much of the time – but extremely reluctant to comply - he was intent on returning to the cockpit. Jim was no stranger to big accidents, but none had hurt him like this one.

Drag racer Kenny Bernstein fielded a team at Indianapolis for the first time in 1988, and had tremendous faith in Jim's ability, bravery and powers of recovery. It would have been easy to fill his seat with a fully fit driver, and one who would bring money too. Jim was never a sponsor-chaser. A potential ride at the 500 is invariably oversubscribed with applicants, a mixture of seasoned pros, rookies and dreamers. Bernstein knew of Jim's outstanding work in developing the Buick stock-block V6 for the 500, and there could be no better man for the job of driving one of his cars in the May classic.

Nothing came easy in Jim's career, apart from the art of driving itself. His Indianapolis comeback had been no different. Rumours on race day morning suggested temperatures could rival the near unbearable highs of May 30th, 1953. That had been the day Bill Vukovich stamped his authority on the event, driving without relief to win his first 500. Meanwhile, Carl Scarborough stumbled from his car and was taken to the infield care centre with a temperature of 103.6 Fahrenheit (39.8 Celsius). While Vukovich was still on his way to victory, Scarborough's life ebbed away, despite desperate efforts to save him.

In 1988 Jim didn't only have the heat to contend with. Metal screws in his leg worked loose during the race, an unwanted distraction at 200mph plus. His race was hardly a cakewalk either. Jim led for seven laps around half distance, but unscheduled pitstops later ruled out the top three finish that seemed a distinct possibility at one point. In total Jim's Lola spent more than six minutes in the pits, including a lengthy stop to cure a transmission fluid leak, and a heart-breaking late tyre change, during which his mechanics wrestled despairingly with a stuck front left wheelnut. To put it into context, winner Mears spent just one minute, 42 seconds in the pits during the race.

Despite all of these frustrations, Jim was happy with his lot. It was easily his best finish at the Brickyard, and a definite improvement over 1987's outcome. Throughout his 500 career – but on that day in particular – the American crowd took the quiet Scotsman to their hearts. Indianapolis

fans have always rooted for the underdog, or those drivers and teams clearly battling adversity. Sportsmanship is also a trait held in high regard at the Speedway. They cheered Ralph de Palma in 1912 as he, along with riding mechanic Rupert Jeffkins, pushed their grey Mercedes home to complete 199 laps, having led 196 laps and been within two of victory. In 1963 Scotsman Jim Clark endeared himself to the Hoosiers with his conduct and driving throughout the month. Many thought he was robbed of victory, due to partisan officials refusing to black flag leader Parnelli Jones, who was trailing oil. With Jim, there was no controversy. He was one of the first to congratulate Jones on his triumph, an act which sat well with those in attendance. Then there was the crowd's perennial hero for many years, Jim Hurtubise. Known as 'Herc' (after Hercules), he was handicapped by severe burns sustained in a 1964 crash. Nobody could doubt his courage, as he attacked Indianapolis's four corners in spectacular fashion every time he was on track. Until 1981 he returned in an increasingly futile bid to qualify his Mallard, a front-engined roadster design which had been made redundant by rear-engine cars in the mid-1960s. He never won the 500, but few have drawn as much admiration.

I only became aware of Jim as an 11-year-old, through the pages of *Autosport* magazine, and towards the end of his career. My interest stemmed initially from the fact that he came from Dunfermline, a town near the village of Crossgates, where I grew up in Fife, Scotland. I became enamoured with the Indianapolis 500. The history, names and mores that surrounded it. As a kid from semi-rural Scotland, it appeared so glamorous and dangerous that it may as well have taken place on Mars.

In 2009, through the wonders of the internet, I made the acquaintance of racing photographer David Hutson, while researching an article for the *Dunfermline Press* about Jim. David provided me with my first real insights into Jim's character, and the more I learned of him the more I liked. After some prodding from David I decided to write a book about Jim, although I still knew comparatively little about his career. After discovering the Crawford family had moved to Bolton when Jim was still very young, I wrote a letter to *The Bolton News*, asking for anyone who remembered Jim to get in touch. The result was overwhelming. Within 24 hours of my letter being published I had around 20 emails from people wishing to share their memories.

I had never written a book before and, as someone who won't even read the instructions on how to wash a jumper, I forged ahead having taken no advice, and with not much of a clue as to what I was doing! It became a stop-start affair, as

> Jim didn't only have the heat to contend with. Metal screws in his leg worked loose during the race, an unwanted distraction at 200mph plus

I struggled to find some crucial people. Locating Mike Peers was a major breakthrough, as he accompanied Jim on a sojourn to Switzerland, which was a period in his life I knew next to nothing about.

In 2017 I finally self-published my book, an A5 softback with a handful of photographs. The response somewhat took me aback, as the print run of 300 sold out in a matter of weeks. This undoubtedly said infinitely more about the popularity of Jim than it did about me. Reviews were very complimentary, but I knew I had unfinished business. In early 2018 I returned to Bolton and carried out more interviews. In early 2020, Covid struck, and it seemed the world was put on hold. It is therefore immensely rewarding to see Jim's story finally being published after the tribulations of the last couple of years.

Jim was a very quotable driver, and you will find the following pages spread liberally with examples of his inciteful, and often humorous, comments. It would, of course, have been wonderful to sit with Jim and write his life story, although several friends have assured me that he would have been embarrassed and bemused by all the fuss. This is not a book detailing chassis numbers and tyre compounds, for I feel Jim would not have been terribly interested in recalling such minutiae. It features cars, of course, but it is fundamentally about Jim the person. Taking the reader from Scotland to England, Trinidad to Canada, India to the US, Jim's story is one lived at full speed in every respect. If it was a stage play it would be impossible to categorise. Part romp, part farce, sometimes tragic and very often comedic.

*Image credit **David Allen Hutson***

Where Jim has spoken on a subject, either on film or in print, I have tended to use his words. There can be no more accurate representation of a person than from listening to what they actually said. Likewise, I tracked down many of Jim's friends, from childhood through to his final years. Having met several of them in person I can say they are wonderful people, who never made me feel anything but extremely welcome. Many knew Jim throughout his life, for he was a loyal friend to those he cared about. Fame did not appear to change him at all and, long after he settled in the US, his old friends in England still received regular phone calls.

This, I hope, is the book that Jim deserves. He had a remarkable career, facing success and adversity with the same easy humour. His story is ultimately tragic, ending prematurely at the age of 54. As his friend Rick Rising-Moore observed, "He sacrificed his body for the sport. There is no question about that." I have no doubt, had Jim lived, he would have been a highly desirable figure to have at classic racing events, where his undemanding manner, patience for fans and vast reserve of stories would have left anyone who met him enthralled. I certainly wish I had met him, and the biggest compliment I received during this endeavour was when one of Jim's friends told me we would have got on well with each other. Despite its tragic ending, this is not a sad story. Jim lived life with verve and enjoyment, squeezing into his 54 years more than many of us can ever hope to. His talent defined his career, not money. Jim was never one comfortable with selling himself to prospective sponsors. His various team bosses showed unerring faith in his abilities, and no one ever doubted his commitment. Why else would his 1985 Indianapolis 500 entrant have staunchly refused to replace Jim – who brought no money with him – with any one of several drivers with considerable financial backing. He loved driving at the limit, and did it whenever he climbed into a car, be it competitive or not.

Many drivers with less talent have achieved more than Jim, in a statistical sense. Statistics aren't always the best gauge of ability however, particularly in a sport with as many variables as motor racing. The great Jim Clark 'only' won two Formula One titles, but few who witnessed the humble Scot's preternatural talent would rate him anything less than the greatest racing driver to ever grace the sport. In Jim Crawford's case, perhaps other drivers have not left the same depth of impression on those whose paths they crossed. One such person is Roman Kuzma, Jim's crew chief for the 1986 Indianapolis 500. "Jim Crawford's infectious grin and optimism, even in the face of adversity, will stay with me forever. In a cut-throat sport that often breeds greed, jealousy and arrogance, Jim was simply a racer's racer. Sometimes the best in a sport doesn't always gain fame, public accolade or championships. Those of us lucky enough to work with Jim received so much more we'll never forget."

I have a signed photo of Jim in my collection from the 1988 Indianapolis 500, a promotional card for the Mac Tools King Racing team. On it he has written the dedication, 'Thanks for making me part of your team.' That perhaps best sums up why Jim was so loved by those he worked with. He never considered himself a superstar driver. He was, above all, a team player.

Jim Crawford touched many lives. He could be humble to the point of shyness, while on track he was often fast to the point of disbelief. Jim's place in the annals of racing history is assured. This is his story.

Chapter One

Fife Born, Lancashire Bred

Jim Crawford was a proud Lancastrian, residing in or around Bolton for more than half of his life. He was, however, born almost 200 miles to the north of the famous mill town. Jim's father, Alexander Crawford, met Annie Shuttleworth at a Bolton dance hall in the late 1930s. 'Alex' was originally from Glasgow, but moved south to Bolton to work for the architectural firm Bradshaw, Gas and Hope in 1936. Married shortly after the outbreak of the Second World War, the couple soon found themselves heading back to Alex's homeland. The couple's first child, a daughter called Jean, was born in Paisley in 1944. "Dad worked on the fake town outside Glasgow to divert enemy bombers away from the city," recalls Jean. "He was sent back to Scotland during the war. My dad's parents originally came from the island of Little Colonsay. They were forced to leave for the mainland by the Highland Clearances."

The Crawfords were living in Fife, at 33 Park Road, Rosyth, by the time James Alan Crawford entered the world on February 13th, 1946. Jim, as he would be known throughout his life, was born at the maternity hospital in nearby Dunfermline. Once the capital city of Scotland, Dunfermline is perhaps best known as the birthplace of the industrialist and philanthropist, Andrew Carnegie.

Rosyth, on Scotland's east coast, is dominated by the large naval dockyard built there at the beginning of the twentieth century. The dockyard became a prime target for the Luftwaffe, as was the Forth Bridge a little to the east. The magnificent Victorian cantilever structure carries trains to this day over the Firth of Forth, between the Lothians and Fife, providing a crucial transport link. The river was heavily defended by anti-aircraft batteries during wartime, and the skies above Rosyth were the setting for the very first air battle of the war, in September, 1939. Today, the bridge is a Category A UNESCO World Heritage Site, giving it the highest level of statutory protection.

Jim spent the first four years of his life in Rosyth before the family moved again, this time back to Bolton permanently. Alex accepted a role working for Nuclear Energy at their highly classified headquarters in Risley. Given his brief

Jim's mother and father, Annie and Alexander. **Boardman Family**

stay in Scotland it is hardly surprising that Bolton would always be where Jim considered home.

Jim and his cousin, Jeff Shuttleworth, grew up as close friends, and their mutual love of thrill-seeking and adventure saw the pair get in several scrapes. Jeff remembers one such occasion, which could have ended in tragedy. "We were at Southport, where Jim and myself were digging caves in the sand. Auntie Annie – Jim's mum – shouted, 'Come on boys, the sandwiches are ready.' I started heading back, but Jim hadn't heard. Then I heard a soft thud behind me. Jim's cave had collapsed on him, and he was buried. I managed to pull him out by his ankles. It was a lucky escape."

The boys actively sought to make any pastime more hazardous than it should be, as Jeff recalls. "We played some dangerous games. We would make bows and arrows from bamboo. By splitting the bamboo a bit we could insert four inch nails in. Then we would fire them at the few wide enough trees down near the Croal River, which ran between the posh-ish Crompton Way area and the roughish Breightmet area, where I grew up. We'd hide behind each tree while the other took aim, and enjoy the thrwang as the nail sank into the wood, instead of into Jim or I! Wild, but bloody exciting! Another time, I was playing darts with Jim. Just as I was getting my last dart out from the board Jim threw one and pinned me to it by the skin between my fingers. I still have the scar to prove it!"

The family's favoured holiday destination was Abersoch, on the Welsh coast. Jeff remembers an event there which appeared to predict both of their futures. "Jim's mum and dad picked me up to take me with them for the third year. It was raining like never before, so they decided to take us to Abersoch village, and to treat us to whatever we liked at the local shop. It was an Aladdin's cave, selling everything from the *Daily Mail* to knickerbocker glories and fishing tackle. Jim and I were told to choose something special. He chose a three-inch-long racing car, and I selected a plastic Frido football. Of course, Jim went on to have his racing career, and I was a professional footballer for a while." Jim clearly did have an interest in racing, even at such a young age. "He would create tracks and ask his dad to buy him Dinky cars."

> Jim's cave had collapsed in on him, and he was buried. I managed to pull him out by his ankles. It was a lucky escape

The Crawfords were a close family, and Jim adored his parents. Friend Richard Cort once asked him about a certain routine he had when he was older. "Jim took his washing every Friday to his parents. 'I'm capable of doing it. I just want to make sure they are alright.'" Jim attended Isis School in Sharples, now demolished. He always loved being around water, and would spend his spare time constructing rafts with friends at a nearby lake, and dreaming of becoming a frogman. At the age of eight or nine Jim first discovered what was to become, arguably, the greatest passion of his life. He became a member of Belmont Sailing Club, a little to the north of Bolton. It was there that Janet Donnison first met him. "We were about 15, and Jim crewed for my brother on occasion. He put the same energy into this as he did into driving. So much so that, one day, he threw himself across the boat as they changed tack, missed the toe straps and went over the side! My brother had to go back for him. Belmont was a place he always went back to."

Jim's obsession with sailing continued throughout his teens. It also led to a legendary story, concerning the purchase of a new boat from Dorset. Rod Lee was with Jim at the time, and an eyewitness to the mayhem which unfolded. The two became friends after seeing each other socially in bars around Bolton.

"Being in the Merchant Navy I would be away for long stretches, but we always used to catch up. I was with him when he set off the sprinkler system in a London car park. We were on our way back with his dad's car after picking up a boat he had bought, and decided to enjoy the London nightlife. This was the swinging '60s! The mast of this thing stuck out over the roof of the car and, when Jim drove down the ramp into the car park, it ripped into the roof and triggered the sprinklers. Well, there were all sorts of nice cars in there, and it was the height of summer. We watched in horror as Rollers with their tops down got flooded! The two of us were dragged into a security guard's office, with Jim in tears. It cost his insurance company a fortune. Anyway, we stayed in a hotel and headed home the following day, only for the trailer to break on the Coventry bypass. We had to go back for it the day after with another trailer we'd borrowed."

Despite this mishap Jim showed great promise, and may well have developed into a top-class competitive sailor, had it not been for a lack of finance. The highlight of his sailing career was finishing third in a national championship event. His friend, Richard Sproston, certainly recognised his talent. "I think that's where he got some of his car control from, because he could control those boats."

With sailing proving to be prohibitively expensive Jim looked for a cheaper sport to pursue and, astonishingly, settled on motor racing! To fund his new hobby the boat had to go. The money raised paid for a Mini Cooper S, replacing the standard version he had been using as a tow car. Jim had already sampled rallying at the wheel of a Mini borrowed from Phil Davies. During an event in Wales he used it to great destructive effect, comprehensively demolishing a wall which acted as a flood defence for a nearby village. Torrential rain followed a short time later, leaving some very disgruntled locals. It was a story Jim loved to tell, and

Jim's mother at Lake Windermere in 1930. It would become a favourite location for Jim to go sailing. **Boardman Family**

A studio shot of Jim as a toddler, with his big sister Jean. **Boardman Family**

Jim loved the water and is seen here looking every inch the young skipper.
Boardman Family

perhaps somewhat embellish.

With his own Mini Jim competed in several events, the most notable being the 1968 Gulf International Rally. This car had been rebuilt after being heavily damaged in a collision with a lamppost. Phil Hargreaves, a neighbour from Crompton Way, served as navigator.

"Right from first learning to drive Jim could easily find the fastest way round any corner without crashing – it was just a fraction slower than the time when he did crash! There are, of course, a few drawbacks to this method, and Jim bent plenty of cars in the process. Not all of them his own! However, I was with him on one occasion when his fast thinking and sharp reactions saved a child's life, when they walked out in front of us, and set against that a few bent cars don't matter very much."

The duo attracted some local media attention, with the *Bolton Evening News* previewing their effort. Jim was described in the article as a car salesman – he was most probably working for Tom Ashton at the time, a garage owner who would soon come to play a part in his young employee's fledgling racing career. With the engine capacity of their challenger increased from 1071cc to 1098cc Jim was buoyantly optimistic

> I was with him on one occasion when his fast thinking and sharp reactions saved a child's life

about their chances, while obviously aware of his 'leave no margin' approach to driving. "I reckon our biggest problem will be keeping the car in one piece. Our aim will be to finish and, if we do, we should be in with a chance of an award because there will not be anything much quicker in our class."

The rally started and finished at the Excelsior Hotel near Manchester Airport, and lasted four days. The gruelling 2000-mile route included a visit to Scotland, but the rally ended in disappointment for Jim. It wasn't an accident which forced his retirement this time, but a broken alternator. The Mini's career ended for good the following year, against a tree on the Express and Star Rally.

Jim's love of high-speed driving wasn't confined to organised events, and hair-raising accounts abound of the budding racing driver on the open road. Sue Deakin was Jim's long-term girlfriend, and often experienced his antics. "We were at Ainsworth with Jim driving, my brother in the back and me in the front. My brother was very excited at the prospect of being driven by a racing driver. We hit a ninety-degree left-hand bend too fast. The car spun around and went backwards up a driveway. 'Yeah, great!' my brother was shouting, while I had been thinking *Oh shit!* On another occasion I remember him turning up at a party, having turned Vera the Volvo (Jim's name for his car) upside down on the way there. He then formed a conga line and danced everyone along to the wreck!"

Rod Lee suffered as a result of Jim's driving, but in a different way. "I got myself a brand new MGB. I decided to do the hippy thing and tour Europe. Jim asked if he could borrow the car while I was away. When I got back Jim came to see me. 'Got some bad news for you,' he said. 'Your car's blown up.' I ended up having to get a job working nights in a bakery to pay for a new engine!" Jim's own dad even fell victim to this ploy. Believing his son was using the vehicle as transport for a night out he was somewhat perturbed to discover that he had actually competed in a rally with it! Although there was steam emanating from it when returned Alex thought it started much better afterwards.

Charles Boardman, Jim's brother-in-law, also paid the price for his generosity on one occasion. Like Lee, he fell for Jim's persuasiveness. "Jim had an old Volvo 145, and I had just bought a new Volvo 245. He asked if he could borrow mine to go and pick up an engine. I gave him the keys and he said he would have it back to me the next day. True to his word, he brought it back the next day, with steam coming out of it. He had been to Pau in France to get the engine!"

Jim not offering to pay for a new engine was not a reflection of his character. He just never seemed to have any money, as Janet Donnison recalls.

Jim is bottom left in this school football team photo. It was a sport he didn't care for. Certainly, his cousin, Jeff Shuttleworth, was surprised such a photo existed. "I didn't think he'd kicked a football in his life!" **Boardman Family**

"It's true that he used to walk into a pub, take a few coins out – not enough for a drink – look around, and ask, 'Anyone want a drink?' Of course, someone else always got them in. But I remember him telling me one night that he would love to be able to buy beautiful presents for the people he loved. At that time he didn't have any money."

With his rally career curtailed Jim sought excitement elsewhere. A sailing trip to East Africa was arranged, and then cancelled as the skipper of the boat changed his plans. Having enthusiastically broadcast details of the trip to friends Jim was eager not to lose face. "I decided that I'd got to go somewhere because I'd told everyone I was going to sail round the world, or something – so I jumped on the next boat to America."

Jim's friend, Jeff Axford, joined him on what was to prove quite an adventure. To begin with the the pair were upgraded to first class from their cabin, "in the bilges" as Jim described it, who had 'borrowed' someone's National Insurance number for the purposes of the trip. This good fortune came about due to maintenance being carried out on their part of the ship. They probably couldn't believe their luck when they were befriended by a wealthy family from the Bahamas, who invited Jim and Jeff to stay with them for a while. Needless to say, with no ties back home, the duo accepted the offer. In the end 'a while' turned out to be six months. From there they headed to Florida. Jim

and Jeff passed a year in the States by working a variety of jobs, including a very convenient engagement delivering cars to various parts of the country, allowing them to move around at someone else's expense. There was also a brief time spent working at a filling station, which was held up at gunpoint!

Eventually, they made it to Los Angeles, where they stayed in a hotel while working 10 to 12 hour days, "playing with computers and bits and bobs." Jim kept in touch

Looking rather awkward in a family wedding shot. Jim was rarely seen in formal wear. **Boardman Family**

18

with home through lengthy letters, which were laced with questions about friends, and his famous, wry humour. They also indicated that his number one sporting interest at this time in his life remained sailing.

Hello again, hope you are all still well and it's not too cold yet. Nothing much happening here. Had an earthquake here Sat morning, just about the time Brocky (Mike Brockbank) got married. Suppose it might be a bad omen. A hotel down the street got burned down today, killed about 10 people I think. Very spectacular. Am still working hard and saving my money. Might even save enough to get back one of these days... Not bothered to be a film star yet. John Wayne's boat tied up just down the jetty from us but don't think he has noticed me yet. Got a couple of letters from John Rainford last week, seems to be OK. Gave me the list of everyone getting married etc... Seems everyone is giving up... Could you send me a copy of the magazine Yachts and Yachting or Yachting World or something like that. I want to read up on the yachts in England and the prices of them. We are still in this hotel and will be here for a bit yet I suppose, as it's pretty reasonable and we don't have the responsibility of an apartment to keep up.

Jim was clearly enamoured by America, and perhaps this early trip planted the seed for his later career move stateside. LA must have seemed like a different planet compared to the grey colours of Bolton he had left.

We are getting used to the action of LA now at night. It is unbelievable. Searchlight up in the sky going round, helicopters all over the place and huge freeways all over the place with all the traffic doing 70mph. The Yanks certainly do everything in a big way.

The price of appliances and the music of the day also merited comment.

That record by Free is out here now, and one by The New Seekers "Look What They've Done To My Song." I know the girl that sings that, Eve Graham from M/C [Manchester]. I think that's the only English record out here. There doesn't seem to be a top 20. They just bash them all out on about 6 radio stations 24hrs a day. The most popular now I think is Simon & Garfunkel "I'd rather be a hammer than a nail" or something. Very catchy tune. It's no wonder everyone has colour TV here. For a 23" brand new they are only £40 and some firms give you a portable black & white tele free with that for the same price. Radios only cost about £1 for a portable as well. It's a pity they are 110 volts or I could smuggle a few home for a profit. Anyway I will close now. Got to get up early for work with the aid of my alarm clock. Cheerio for now, Jim
P.S. Don't forget my magazines.

A rare shot of Jim during his brief and spectacular rally career. He doesn't appear to have yet acquired a crash helmet. **Keith Humphreys**

With no visa to work in America it was only a matter of time before the authorities caught up with the pair, and in July, 1970, they did. A brief stay in jail was the result before they hastily left the country for England, via Nassau and Luxembourg. Jim would later tell friend Richard Cort that they had to stand in line all day for water when incarcerated, and that it was so dry their jeans disintegrated. He remarked, "If there's one thing I've learned in life, it is never, ever put yourself in jail."

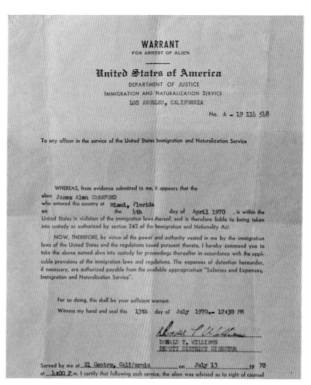
Warrant for Jim's arrest, issued in April, 1970. It took until July for the authorities to find him. **Boardman Family**

Chapter Two

A Helping Hand

An early single-seater outing for Jim in Steve Choularton's Alexis 15 Formula Ford, seen here fending off Geoff Lees. Both men would go on to reach Formula One. **Boardman Family**

Back home, Jim settled into his favoured pastimes of socialising and drinking in and around Manchester. On one night out he made the acquaintance of Charlie Choularton, whose brother, Steve, would soon play a significant role in Jim's life. The Choulartons were successful bankers in the city, and lived in a grand old house where parties were commonplace. 'Fess' Parker remembers it well. "Charlie had this huge basement in his house where we used to go. It consisted of tanks full of strange reptiles, lots and lots of booze and a record player in the corner." Steve Choularton soon got to know Jim as well. "Jim came along with his friend, John Rainford, to enjoy the south Manchester nightlife, in which my family home, Graythwaite, seemed to play a significant role. We were all big drinkers, and girl chasers, and we got friendly."

Rod Lee also knew Charlie and Steve, and was a visitor to their infamous basement. "The Choulartons employed a full-time falconer. In their basement they had piranha, snapping turtles and various other creatures. There was also an old, blind pitbull which walked into all the furniture." Richard Jones, who would go on to a stellar career in sports car racing, was around the Choulartons at the same time. "I went to sixth-form college with the Choularton brothers at Hale Barns. They invited me swimming one day. We were waiting in between two bus stops, when a Rolls-Royce pulled up and took us to their house. They had a swimming pool and butlers. Charlie was a wonderful, wild character, but not interested in motor racing."

Steve Choularton was very interested in motor racing, and became increasingly friendly with Jim. Of particular interest to Jim was an Alexis Mk15 Formula Ford owned by his new acquaintance. Steve had acquired the car from legendary Manchester racing car dealer Bob Howlings, and it required considerable work before it could be driven. Choosing his moment carefully – when Steve was somewhat inebriated at a party – Jim came to an agreement with him. He would be allowed to try the car out if he helped repair it. Jim later recalled the struggles he had, along with a friend, to achieve this. "We hadn't a clue what it was all for. Roll bars and wishbones we didn't know what to do with – we couldn't work out what the bits were and which way they were up." When the single-seater was finally completed Jim took it for a maiden test drive on Crompton Way, in the snow!

At this time Jim had steady employment, working at a local garage owned by Tom Ashton. His duties there included delivering cars to customers, including a Ford Anglia which he wrote off on the way to its owner. Despite this, Ashton was sympathetic towards Jim's motor racing ambitions. In exchange for occasionally displaying the Alexis in the showroom window Ashton agreed to sponsor Jim in Formula Ford. "I kitted him out, and picked up the tab when he went off through the hoardings! I swear he must have had eight wheels on the car, as he went through quite a number of tyres."

Jim's friend, Rod Crompton, accompanied him to Croft on one occasion. It was to prove far from straightforward.

OFFICIAL PROGRAMME **10p**

MOTOR RACE MEETING

ORGANISED BY
THE BRITISH AUTOMOBILE RACING CLUB

CROFT AUTODROME

SUNDAY
9th MAY
1971

Numerical List of Competitors—continued

No.	Name	Car	c.c.	Colour	Town
101	(Driver: Malcolm Wayne) Tate of Leeds Titan FF	1600	Red/Violet	Leeds	
102	(Driver: Chris Meek) Nick Done Alexis Mk.18	1600	Red/Silver	Bolton	
103	Ian Beresford Palliser FF	1600		Chesterfield	
104	Neil Ginn Lotus 69F	1600	White	Helensburgh	
105	Bob Prest Dulon LD4	1600	Yellow	Croxdale	
106	Terry Horrocks Alexis Horrocks	1600	Yellow	Preston	
107	John Hamilton Merlyn Mk.20	1600	Blue	Sheffield	
108	Ken Bailey Titan Mk.6	1600	Orange/White	Stretford	
109	Ted Payne Lotus 51	1600	Orange	Middleton	
110	Jim Crawford Alexis Mk.15	1600	Orange/White	Bolton	
111	Jeremy Gambs Lotus 61M	1600	Silver/Red	Farnham	
112	Chris Spencer-Phillips Palliser FF	1600	Yellow	Chelmsford	
113	Bernard Hunter Jnr. Hawke DL 2A	1600	Yellow	Leith	
114	Dave Manners Alexis Mk.15	1600	Purple/Gold	Darlington	
115	Chris Tipping March 708	1600	Red	Ilkley	
126	Robert Leckie Hillman Imp	998		Aberdeen	
127	Andy Barton B.L. Cooper S	999	Blue/White	Newcastle	
128	Bob Parkinson B.L. Cooper S	999	Blue/White	Melbourne	
129	(Driver: Ron Warren) Sedric Bell B.L. Cooper	999	Blue/Red	Carlisle	
130	David Lyon B.L. Cooper	998	Heliotrope	Hull	
131	Kay Raper B.L. Cooper S	999	White/Yellow	Cottingham	
132	Owen Corrigan B.L. Cooper S	999	Green	Blackhall	
133	Christopher Robinson B.L. Cooper	998	White/Red	Darlington	
134	David Ewart B.L. Cooper	998	Blue/Orange	Hull	
135	Jim Howden Chrysler Coupe	998	Yellow/White	Edinburgh	
136	George Hard B.L. Mini Clubman	984	White/Blue	Wilmslow	
137	Michael Lightfoot B.L. Cooper S	998	Blue	Sunderland	
154	Graham Gerrard B.L. Mini	850	Purple/White	Huddesfield	
155	Peter Dzierzek Lola T55	1650	White	Kirkliston	
156	Bob Howlings Lola 5000/142 Chev	5000	Green	Manchester	
158	Max Reinhard Kincraft Ford	4700	Blue	York	
159	Bill Wood Brabham 5000 Traco	5000	Blue	Lilling	
165	Bob Howlings Chevron B17C	1600	Red	Manchester	
166	(Driver: Nick May) Alida-Else Racing Team Lotus 59FA B.D.A.	1600	Yellow	Codnor	
176	(Driver: Chris Oates) John Finch Chevron F3 Ford	997	Blue/Gold	Chesterfield	
177	Keith Wright Brabham BT27 Ford	997	Red/Black	Dewsbury	
178	John Coulter Brabham BT28 Ford	998	Orange	York	

Left and above: Jim overcame adversity just to make it to Croft Autodrome. By the time the circuit closed ten years later he would be the outright lap record holder. **Boardman Family**

"The car was put in an old furniture van, with a mechanic and myself. Meanwhile, Jim was driving his dad's car there. Just past Bolton Wanderers' ground the van's oil pressure dropped. It was knackered. Jim said to me, 'Rod, you've got an old Land Rover pick-up.' So, he drove me to get it while he went and collected a trailer he'd quickly arranged to borrow. By the time we got to Croft we'd missed practice. Jim started at the back and retired on lap three with ignition problems. We got home late and got drunk, but he would overcome great problems just to race."

In total Jim competed in ten Formula Ford races, but it was a largely frustrating foray into the world of single-seaters, although Jim did win his class in a Libre race at Oulton Park. He would later go on to become something of a folk hero at the circuit. Jim hadn't actually won on the road, but was promoted to first when Allen Karlberg received a penalty. "That was my first prize money and I was over the moon. I was all ready for my first house in Switzerland."

Steve Choularton had also been racing Formula Ford, but for 1971 chose to buy an Alexis Mk17 with which to compete in the new Formula Atlantic series. After a disastrous campaign Jim talked his friend into purchasing a Lotus 69 for 1972. He assisted Choularton with the preparation of the Lotus throughout the year, and as a reward was allowed to drive it in a Libre race at Croft that autumn. It was this race which first really gave people an indication of Jim's talent, battling with the experienced and quick Tony Dean. He recalled the day in an *Autosport* interview. "Tony Dean won it, with me right up his boot the whole way – I was quite pleased with that."

Jim's outstanding performance at Croft wasn't quite the first time he had been behind the wheel of the 69. Richard Jones recalls an earlier occasion. "The first time I met Jim was at a test day at Croft. I was there with my 998cc Mini, and he was helping Steve with his Atlantic. Steve was struggling to get the set-up right. Jim jumped in, after borrowing Steve's helmet. He did an out lap, flying lap and in-lap. Jim then made changes to the ride height, roll bar and suspension, went out and was much quicker."

At season's end the Lotus was swapped for an Alfa Romeo road car, and Choularton purchased a March 73B with which to have another crack at Atlantic. Jim went with him to Paul Ricard in the south of France for some pre-season testing with the March team. Choularton still has vivid memories of the trip. "Harvey Postlethwaite was the engineer at the time, a very impressive man. Hans Stuck was testing the F2 car and Mark Donohue was down there with the Porsche Can Am monster, the 917/30. Jim was a funny guy. We were in our hotel and all the electricity went off. Hans Stuck walked in through the front door with his German crew and Jim said, 'Many Hans makes light work.' Coincidentally, the light came on just at that point in time!"

On June 10th, 1973, Jim was once again unleashed around

Jim's first sponsor was his employer, garage owner Tom Ashton. Keith Humphreys to the right. **Keith Humphreys**

Sitting in the cockpit of Steve Choularton's Lotus 69 in Crompton Way. Jim made quite an impression at Croft with this car. **Keith Humphreys**

Croft, in a round of the BRSCC (British Racing & Sports Car Club) Northern Single-Seater Championship. He went one better than in 1972 and won the race, lapping everyone bar Roger Craven in a Formula Three GRD, who was still a minute behind. Chris Mason was full of praise for the thoroughly unexpected winner in *Autosport*. "Crawford had only raced once in the past two years (he chased Tony Dean at Croft last Autumn in Choularton's Lotus 69) yet he went out and, incredibly, shattered Dean's outright lap record, on his way to victory. From the chicane Crawford's driving looked positively breathtaking. After this performance there could be no doubt of the destination of the BMW Concessionaires' Man of the Meeting award."

Paul Carr was working for Bob Howlings at Croft. Although he didn't see much of Jim that day the two would soon become friends. "As a young man I met Jim when he was working as a mechanic for Stephen Choularton. Jim and I would dash up and down the motorway to March Engineering for bits and spares at all times of night and day in a beat-up old van. Three things that we had in common were drinking, girls and motor racing. Our van trips were always full of good humour. Young Jim Crawford found it very hard to be serious at times. He would always laugh at his own jokes, and always had that cheeky grin on his face."

Howlings himself was a well-known character in northern racing circles. If a driver needed a new racing car, or spares, he was the go-to man. He ran his used racing car business from the railway arches at the bottom of Deansgate in Manchester, with a caravan for an office. Ex-Chevron mechanic Kevin Hodgkinson was a regular visitor and remembers that Howlings, "would take anything in part exchange, even livestock!"

Hodgkinson was also at the Croft meeting and remembers the impact Jim made. He raced a Chevron in his spare time, after swapping from two wheels to four some years earlier following a serious accident at the Manx Grand Prix. His parents only became aware of his racing exploits when they were summoned to his hospital bed! "I was racing my Chevron B17 in the Monoposto race and just happened to be

parked next to Jim. We got chatting and discovered that we both came from the same area in Lancashire. He was working on the car, and I thought he was doing the spannering. All he had on were jeans and T-shirt. It was only when I got talking to him I realised he was the driver!"

The two men would go on to become good friends and, when at the same meeting, would try and park next to each other in the paddock. "It was like an ice-breaker, coming from the same area in Lancashire. Jim used to take great delight in annihilating what we called 'southern drivers with money.' There's a lot of class distinction in four-wheel racing, irrespective of how good you are."

Hodgkinson knew John Bridges, part owner of Chevron, from his time working there, and recalls his reaction to Jim's winning drive. "John was very taken with Jim's driving ability. Later in the day he said that, from what he saw, Jim would be an ideal candidate to drive one of their single-seaters."

From this moment on Jim's racing career began to rapidly gain momentum. Shortly after his Croft appearance Jim received a call about driving in Formula Three for GRD. This eventually came to nothing, but he had got to know Neil Edwards, a mechanic who worked for Chevron in Bolton. Chevron designed and built cars for a variety of racing classes, from sports cars to single seaters. The company was founded by Scotsman Derek Bennett in the 1960s, who went from designing and building home-made model aeroplanes as a youngster to designing and building world renowned racing cars as a young man. Edwards had been impressed by reports of Jim's driving from Bridges. Edwards and Jim headed out one Sunday evening to a bar where they knew Bennett would be. The plan worked, and Jim was invited to test for the team on the following Tuesday at Aintree.

Jim's Chevron test proved to be just as impressive as his maiden single-seater race outing. Bennett asked him to go and see him at the factory the following day and made Jim an offer, as recalled by Edwards. "Derek told Jim, 'If you can get an engine and you can find enough bits in the stores Neil will build you a car.'"

Chapter Three

Frantic Atlantic

Charging towards second place and a maiden podium at Oulton Park in October, 1973. **Boardman Family**

dwards built a Formula Atlantic spec B25, but Jim didn't just require a car. Half of the company was owned by John Bridges, who took pity and gifted Jim a crash helmet and set of overalls. The crash helmet was in the traditional Chevron colours of black and yellow. Jim soon adapted it to the design he would keep for the rest of his career, with a thick red stripe running over the top and continuing below the visor.

Jim's Atlantic debut came on September 9th, 1973, at Oulton Park. It was the final round of the Yellow Pages Championship and, while Choularton raced to a fourth-place finish, Jim crashed out on the second lap. Six days later he won a Libre event at Aintree, and on September 22nd Jim was back at Oulton Park for a round of the BP Atlantic championship. Again, an accident put paid to his chances. It was an inauspicious start to his Atlantic career.

Finally, on the last day of September, Jim completed an Atlantic race distance, finishing ninth at Brands Hatch. Next time out at Oulton he was on the podium, finishing runner-up by less than a second to John Nicholson's Lyncar. He could barely believe the situation he found himself in. "I sat there on the front row with all your Nicholsons and

Purleys and thought *Christ, what am I doing here?* You expect to get trampled in the rush when they drop the flag."

Jim's brief season finished with a fifth place at Brands Hatch, and retirement due to gearbox failure from the final BP round at Snetterton. At Brands Hatch, Jim met Mike Peers, someone else who would come to play a major role in his career. "I was at a nearby university at the time. We instantly got on really well. I went to various other races, and I used to see him in Bolton in a pub called Fanny's. Jim was as tight as they came. You'd go into a pub and he'd arrange all his money on the table, 2ps and 1ps. He'd take so long 'coppering up' that someone would always have bought a round by the time he'd finished!"

Jim ended 1973 as joint Formula Atlantic lap record holder at Oulton (shared with John Nicholson). His performances had not gone unnoticed at *Autosport* magazine, with Chris Mason praising Jim's efforts, while lamenting the plight of northern based drivers. "I have a sneaking suspicion that had Jim Crawford's explosive arrival on the scene this year, as a virtual novice driver in Formula Atlantic, taken place at Brands, he would have been lauded far more than he has been so far."

Jim is pictured here at Brands Hatch, where he finished fifth.
Boardman Family

Jim on his Formula Atlantic debut at Oulton Park, not yet sporting his own helmet design. **Alan Cox**

Jim waiting to go out in his March 73B at Brands Hatch. **Boardman Family**

For 1974 Jim would race alongside his friend Choularton under the SDC racing banner. The team was based at the old Red Rose Racing premises in Bolton, and over the winter built up a second March 73B for Jim, which he would christen 'Mary March.' Choularton can remember the naïvety with which they approached single-seater racing. "Now I think back, we did have a mechanic. At least we thought he was, until it came to it. That was the problem initially. You really have no idea what to do to get things to work. Cyd Williams was very helpful. Then we started meeting real mechanics and people like Jeff Goodliff. A deep breath, spend the money, get the right people and things start working."

Tony Griffiths worked for Nicholson McLaren Engines at the time, who were heavily involved in Formula Atlantic. "Jim was always a very quiet bloke. We used to talk maybe once a week, mainly about who and what was going on. He was always too modest about what he had done or was doing."

The 1974 John Player championship opened at Mallory Park on March 10th in miserable conditions, with sleet and rain pounding the Leicestershire circuit. Although the rain had stopped by the time the Atlantics were flagged away, everyone was on wet tyres. Jim qualified seventh, but a demon getaway saw him surge through to second place on lap one, behind John Nicholson's Lyncar. Jim shadowed Nicholson for the entire race, crossing the finish line 0.2 seconds behind. Richard Scott was third, the only man able to stay on the same lap. Jim left Mallory with points on the board and the BP Man of the Meeting award.

One week later the Atlantic boys descended on Brands Hatch, in conditions just as dreary as Mallory. Jim had a weekend to forget, forced out of the race by a wheel bearing failure, while his countryman Scott held on to win by just

over a second. It truly was a case of hanging on for Scott. His lead had been as great as 40 seconds until debris damaged his airbox and entered the engine, seriously impeding its performance.

The poorly supported MCD Formula Atlantic series began at Silverstone on March 31st, where Jim upset the organisers by qualifying in his team-mate's car without informing them. In the race he followed Choularton all the way to the flag, finishing two tenths behind him in sixth position. The SDC Marches ran with new rear wings for round three of the John Player championship at Silverstone, but both drivers struggled with understeer all weekend. The race turned into a frustrating affair for Jim. Early on he ran second, right behind Nicholson. He even made an attempt to pass for the lead around the outside of Woodcote. Nicholson started to experience brake problems, but an overheating engine left Jim in no position to take advantage. He ran the rest of the distance in conservation mode, eventually slipping to fifth position. There was some joy for SDC, with Choularton claiming second place. The race was won comfortably by Tony Brise, who carved through the field after a poor start in his tiny Formula Three March.

The end of April saw Jim finally claim his maiden win in Atlantic, at Oulton Park, in the second MCD race of the season. He started second but took the lead immediately and never relinquished it, despite a leaking oil tank and severe handling problems, which would plague him for much of the season.

With just a few days before the next John Player race, again at Oulton Park, Jim undertook some midweek testing in a bid to cure his handling woes. Despite this he was still finding the March a handful. Throwing the car around Oulton's 1.9 miles Jim claimed a well-earned pole.

> Jim was always too modest about what he had done or was doing

Geoff Friswell may have challenged him, but pushed too hard and crashed. Nicholson was an impressive second in his newly rebuilt and modified Lyncar. The reason for the rebuild was a huge crash during testing, with the car's designer at the wheel. Lining up third was the Wella-sponsored March of amiable American, Ted Wentz, who led into the first corner. It took Jim a dozen laps to get the lead back, but Wentz was not the type to give up easily. "Past the pits the two cars were side by side with the Wella one on the inside. It was a move doomed to failure, as Ted frankly admitted afterwards, and after a few more feet in the lead he ended his race against the bank with a couple of bent corners and complaining of a serious bout of brain fade."

Late in the race Jim had his own problems to deal with. A broken gear linkage on the penultimate lap left him stuck in fourth, but he nursed the car home to a popular victory. Despite his success Jim was still leading a very hand-to-mouth existence. Kevin Hodgkinson remembers that, "in all the time I knew Jim I can't recall him ever saying he had a full time job."

Podium finishes followed at Silverstone and Oulton Park, where Nicholson gained revenge for their May encounter with a very narrow victory. By the time June came around Jim had an inkling that his friend and team-mate was struggling to keep two competitive cars running, and realised a cash injection would be required for him to see out the season. A small article even appeared in *Autosport*, under the headline 'Help Crawford', highlighting his plight. In the same issue Ian Titchmarsh sang Jim's praises, stating that, "he must be Britain's most promising driver outside Formula One."

Before the next John Player round at Mallory Jim managed an afternoon of testing at Silverstone, with March's Robin Herd present to try and diagnose the source of the car's handling issues. At Mallory Jim started from second, having recorded the same lap time as

polesitter Cyd Williams. He took the lead from Nicholson and held on for an impressive victory, despite an assault from Dave Morgan and an uncomfortable final few laps when, "... the March's fire extinguisher discharged into a rather tender, but vital, part of the anatomy with 10 laps to go, giving him some idea of what a brass monkey must feel like at sub-zero temperatures. It seemed to have little effect on his post-race performance!"

To save money Jim skipped the next MCD round at Thruxton, but soon afterwards good news arrived from Max Mosley, who confirmed March would be providing factory support and the loan of a car, thereby making Jim the only works backed driver in Atlantic. In reality the rest of the year would still prove financially difficult and Jim eventually gave the car back to March, preferring his own.

Jim was back in action at Brands Hatch for the most prestigious race of the year, supporting the British Grand Prix. Jim's hopes of shining in front of the Formula One bosses were thwarted in the race by a misfiring engine. Despite this he finished a commendable third, behind Alan Jones and Dave Morgan. The curious handling problem had also resurfaced. It caused the car to oversteer wildly on left-handers, and in practice Jim had crashed as a result. Despite all of this he left Kent with a bigger lead in the championship, having benefited from title rival Nicholson having to pit.

Jim wasn't only driving Atlantics that summer. He also tested a Chevron B25 Formula Two car in late July for Team Harper. This was his second experience of the class, having previously lapped Oulton Park under the F2 lap record time in a works Chevron. There were even rumours for a while that he may replace Dieter Quester in the team. A few weeks later Jim also enjoyed an outing in a Surtees TS15 Formula Two at Goodwood. Influential people were beginning to take notice of his potential.

After missing another MCD round at Silverstone Jim

SDC Racing's transporter and twin March 73Bs at the former premises of Red Rose Racing. **Boardman Family**

Jim lines up on pole at Oulton Park, with John Nicholson for company on the front row. Note the fire marshal in full protective gear. Safety had stepped up a notch throughout the sport after the very public loss of Roger Williamson at Zandvoort in 1973. **Alan Cox**

Formula Atlantic at its best. Jim leads Dave Morgan, John Nicholson and Ted Wentz at Mallory. **Alan Cooper**

Jim was fortunate not to be taken out by an errant Morgan. **Alan Cooper**

week later, where electrical gremlins saw Jim retire from the final after having finished second to Brise in his heat. Nicholson could only manage fifth in the final, but it closed the points gap yet further. The call up then came from Team Harper, and Jim found himself at Nogaro in southwest France, making his Formula Two debut. He performed commendably, finishing the race in fifth position.

Early October saw Jim once again in the news, this time looking for a drive in 1975, as it was clear Choularton would be unable to run both men. "He told us (*Autosport*) last week that he would drive virtually anything that would keep him occupied every weekend. He is most interested in F2 and sports cars."

The penultimate round of the John Player Atlantic series took place at Brands Hatch, and Jim was soon on the back foot after crashing heavily in practice. Exiting Stirling's Bend he tripped over a much slower car. "I got a bit agitated," was his refreshingly honest explanation. Having already qualified on the front row the rules allowed Jim to take over his team-mate's car. A driver could start from their original grid position as long as they were in the same make of car. Despite this a situation unfolded which illustrated Jim's easy-going nature, or naïvety, and possibly both. "Johnny Nicholson raised an objection and immediately Crawford relented and agreed to start from the fourth row, having set that time in the couple of laps he managed in Choularton's car at the end of the session."

At such a critical stage of the season it undoubtedly handed an advantage to Nicholson, who himself would now start from the front row. Despite this, Jim caught up in the race and eventually found a way past the Lyncar, only to allow Nicholson back through when an attempt to overtake Alan Jones didn't work out as planned. Jim muscled past again at Paddock, only to lose the position just a few hundred yards later at Druids. Jones then became an unwitting influence on the title battle, when gear selection problems slowed him at Westfield. Nicholson stayed on

returned to the grid at Mallory, claiming pole. The MCD series had by now gained the backing of Southern Organs. Jim ran second to Nicholson's much revised Lyncar in the race, but the March's handling quickly deteriorated, and he was hard pushed in the end to hold off Dave Morgan's Chevron. The *Autosport* report described Jim's troubles as having "the big Ronnie Petersons" at every corner, comparing him to the great Swede who was a master of oversteer.

By the time of the next John Player round at Mallory Park in late August Jim had a Lotus F1 testing contract in his pocket. Mallory was a weekend to forget, and Jim saw his lead eroded from 23 points to just eight. He led early on, only to spin at the hairpin (probably on fluid from the car of American Wes Dawns, who managed to crash there on the warm-up lap). A bad situation was compounded further when Peter Wardle's Surtees slammed into Jim's stranded car.

The Atlantic caravan journeyed across the Irish sea next. Second place behind Dave Morgan at Phoenix Park was followed by disappointment at Mondello Park one

A relieved Jim celebrates victory after an eventful race at Mallory. **Alan Cooper**

Jim and David Purley were briefly teammates at Team Harper. **Boardman Family**

track, but Jim was forced into avoiding action and slewed onto the grass in avoidance, where his nose cone was ripped off. While he regained the track and nursed the March to second Nicholson finished third to set up a title decider at Oulton with the two tied on points.

The race at Brands had been utterly dominated by Tony Brise in his Modus, aided by a set of Firestones intended for Formula Two. When the championship arrived at Oulton the leading players – by hook or by crook – had all acquired some. They weren't required until the race itself, as practice was a wet affair. Nicholson qualified third, with Jim on the row behind having blown an engine. A similar situation to Brands Hatch then unfolded, with the SDC drivers swapping cars. This thoroughly confused the officials, despite the rules clearly stating such an arrangement was allowed. The matter was finally laid to rest shortly before the start. On a drying track Brise had a rare lapse of concentration and crashed out during the warm-up laps. While Jones disappeared in the lead all the interest lay in the battle between Nicholson and the local hero for fourth position. Jim thought he saw a chance to pass his rival early in the race at the tight Esso curve, only for the two to collide. Jim was out with a broken radiator, while Nicholson's Lyncar was damaged but able to continue. He eventually came home in fifth, enough for the title.

With the John Player championship lost and insufficient funds to make the remaining MCD rounds it looked like being a miserable end to a year that had looked so promising for so long. Salvation arrived in the form of Fred Opert, the US Chevron importer. He elected to run Jim in an ex-Hector Rebaque/Bill Henderson Chevron B27. Having missed four of the eight MCD rounds held so far Jim was a long shot for the title, but things began to go his way at the penultimate round at Snetterton,

> ## Jim was a long shot for the title, but things began to go his way

his first race for Opert. Alan Jones looked set for victory until a very late puncture allowed Jim past, followed by Ted Wentz. The result set up a championship decider at Brands Hatch on November 3rd. With double points being awarded it meant no less than six drivers, in addition to Jim, were in with a mathematical chance of the title. Mallock, Jones, Wentz, Friswell, Nicholson and Morgan all went into the race with high hopes.

Jones claimed pole in a car which had been quickly rebuilt after a heavy practice crash, with points leader Mallock second and Nicholson completing the front row. Jim started from row two but was quickly into third and then eased past Mallock. Jones had opened up a decent lead, but Jim steadily chipped away at it. Still, it did not look like being enough. That was until luck once again deserted Jones late on, this time in the form of a gearbox problem which left him stuck in fourth. Jim passed the Australian easily to take the victory and the title.

The 1974 Atlantic season ended with the non-championship Wella Hair Care Trophy race at Thruxton in mid-November. It was a day of joy for Choularton, who took the victory. Jim – who retired with a broken nosecone – was delighted for his friend, and the pair rounded off the season in unique style. "That was a nice event,

Enjoying the spoils of victory with Gabrielle Drake, sister of musician Nick Drake. **Boardman Family**

and I got to see myself win on time-lapsed TV back in the transporter. Harry Stiller had a massive party at his club in Bournemouth. He had a rather cool single-seater bolted vertically to the wall. Jim and I got very drunk and ended up streaking. Then they left the intercom on in my bedroom so they could broadcast me humping round the hotel."

A prestigious honour came Jim's way, in the form of a Grovewood Award. A judging panel recognised his efforts, and Jim even donned a suit for the ceremony. His year was topped off at a reception in London on December 18th where he was presented with the 'BP Superman of the Year' award. Previous recipients included the late Roger Williamson and Bob Evans.

Jim's parents were understandably proud of his achievements, and his mother kept a scrapbook of his career. They were, like Jim, quite reserved and kept their distance. They would often go to watch him race and pay the full entry fee, while he had no idea they were there.

For the SDC drivers, life was very good indeed. While the racing was treated very seriously there was still ample time away from the track for socialising. Jim had many haunts in and around Manchester. Two of his favourites were Time and Place nightclub and the Griffin pub in Bowden. Their lifestyles were worlds away from the monk-like existence of many modern drivers. Jim enjoyed smoking and wasn't averse to a curry the night before a race. For these impressive young men chasing women was often a priority, but racing was never far from Jim's mind. Choularton recalls a story Jim told of a rather curious evening:

"He went to a wife-swapping party up in Bolton. He didn't have a wife, but as it turned out that didn't matter. It was one of those where everyone threw their car keys into the middle of the table and then you took one and ended up with that person. Jim saw a set of Ferrari keys. He picked them up, slipped out of the party and spent the rest of the evening thrashing it. At least that's his story!"

It wasn't just away from the track that Jim enjoyed indulging in high jinks, as an episode Choularton remembers demonstrates. "He didn't have much concern about safety. We were at Mondello Park once and Bev Bond took Jim out for a lap in a road car. At the hairpin Jim surreptitiously reached down and yanked the handbrake

Jim waits on the grid at Thruxton in a Fred Opert Chevron B27. **Boardman Family**

on. Of course, Bev's car spun. Bev didn't know what had happened and Jim couldn't stop laughing."

Janet Donnison also fell victim to her friend's devilish sense of humour behind the wheel, this time on a public road. "I often drove Jim about – not that he was very complimentary about my driving – and I suffered the handbrake turn trick, on a dark country road as we headed to a party. On another occasion we left the sailing club to go back to a friend's house. Jim was driving the friend's Triumph Stag, and I was in an old Escort. 'Follow me!' he said, 'I know a short cut.' Well, in my attempt to keep up I finished in a hedge. When I finally arrived at the house Jim was outside, on the point of coming to look for me. When he saw the slight damage and bits of grass hanging off the bumper he nearly split his sides laughing."

Being presented with a very welcome cheque as part of his Grovewood Award for 1974. **Boardman Family**

Chapter Four

Brief Encounters of the F1 Kind

Jim's Atlantic performances had made him a hot property by the summer of 1974. Remarkably, given the brevity of his career so far, Formula One beckoned. The Surtees and Lotus teams were both interested in securing Jim's services. Mike Peers also recalls a phone call from Ken Tyrrell around the same time. Jim turned to his Atlantic team-mate and trusted friend for advice. As Choularton recalls, their decision-making process was rather unconventional:

"Jim and I were as thick as thieves, so I knew all the details about the F1 offers. We used to rate them by how much whisky you had to drink before you made your mind up. Surtees didn't require a drink. It was very flattering but even we knew that without the right machinery you couldn't get anywhere. Truth is, we were very worried about Lotus. We rated it a one-bottle-of-whisky problem. They had the habit of signing up promising drivers but not giving them a regular drive. Once signed up no-one else was interested so you lost all those opportunities you would never hear of."

Paddy Atkinson also remembers Jim telling him about the Surtees offer. "He told Jim to come over for a word, and not to sign with anyone else until he'd seen him. Of course, in the meantime, Jim signed for Lotus. He still went and saw Surtees, who wasn't happy. Jim said his words to him were, 'You'll never drive in this country again!'"

The SDC pair's thoughts on Lotus would turn out to be painfully prophetic, but for the moment it seemed a tantalising chance to break through into the big league. Jim was summoned to meet Chapman, and duly signed as a test driver. After less than one full season in single-seater racing Jim Crawford was a Formula One driver. Upon his return home Jim filled Choularton in on the most important appointment of his life to date:

"He gave me a blow-by-blow account of the Lotus meeting. They entertained him with stories about the determination of Jim Clark and Graham Hill. The story was they both used to pogo up and down the stairs at Colin's house and they would have eating competitions. They would put out those wobbly custard melbas on a table and see how many they could eat without using their hands. This was meant to inspire Jim to greater heights of determination. He found the whole thing quite amusing."

Jim's new-found fame was difficult for him to comprehend, a fact which came across in an interview with David Gordon in 1974. "I'd like to have tea with the Mayor – when I'm world champion. I hope you're not taking all this I'm saying seriously. I'm just making it up as I go along. I feel as though I've got to make it all glamorous... I don't seem to fit into the image of what I think a racing driver is... but I don't suppose it matters – does it?"

Lotus founder Colin Chapman had long been a champion of young British talent. This no doubt had its roots in the extraordinary success he enjoyed throughout much of the 1960s with Jim Clark. Chapman had identified the potential of the introverted Scottish sheep farmer early, and if the car lasted the distance Clark was usually unbeatable. He won more than one third of the Formula One World Championship Grands Prix he started, in an era of much poorer reliability than today. Like Jim Crawford he was born in Fife, and also competed at the Indianapolis 500. Clark won the American classic in 1965, and came frustratingly close on two other occasions.

Clark's death during a Formula Two race in April 1968 devastated Chapman and Lotus. He tried other young British drivers in his cars over the following seasons with little success. Mike Spence was killed one month to the day after Clark, when a Lotus he was trying out for another driver crashed at Indianapolis. Jackie Oliver, Richard Attwood and John Miles also appeared for Lotus in Formula One, but failed to win a race. Oliver debuted in the aftermath of Clark's death, having only competed in one grand prix, and that in the Formula Two class. He described it as an "impossible task, to fill the seat of the greatest driver in the world" and was relieved to move to BRM. Lotus was hit by further tragedy in 1970 when Austrian driver Jochen Rindt perished at Monza during qualifying for the Italian Grand Prix. In the subsequent races no driver managed to overhaul Rindt's points total and he therefore became F1's first, and only, posthumous world champion.

Rindt's death aside, the early part of the '70s was a golden period for Lotus. The team won two drivers' titles, albeit with foreign drivers. Brazilian Emerson Fittipaldi was champion in 1972. Both Rindt and Fittipaldi won their titles in Chapman's Lotus 72, a revolutionary car which first appeared in 1970. By the time Jim arrived on the scene in 1975 it was still in use, heavily modified and not particularly competitive. Jim described his time as a Lotus Formula One test driver in typically down to earth manner. "My job was basically to drive the thing round and round, banging

*Jim's crash helmet now featured JPS sponsorship, which brought some material benefits. **Alan Cox***

*Jim being interviewed by well known MCD circuit commentator Anthony Marsh at Mallory Park. **Author's collection.***

*Jim jumped at the opportunity to sample Geoff Wood's Escort Supersaloon between his single-seater commitments. **Geoff Werran***

over kerbs until something fell off."

Jim's initial outing in a Formula One car was in the much-maligned Lotus 76. Introduced in 1974 it soon became apparent the design was fundamentally unsound, resulting in the ageing 72 being called back into action. Jim drove Peterson's 76 at Snetterton at the end of the summer in 1974. He quickly impressed team manager Peter Warr by managing to identify a brake problem on the car and set solid lap times. Chapman and Warr briefly flirted with the idea of giving Jim a car for the season-ending US Grand Prix at Watkins Glen, before deciding he was perhaps just a little too inexperienced.

Before the 1975 season started Jim travelled to Florida with Derek Bennett. The purpose of their trip was to generate sales for the new B29 through American Chevron agent Fred Opert. Jim did a sterling job in demonstrating the potential of the car, lapping the circuit at West Palm Beach over two seconds quicker than the existing record held by a Formula 5000 car. Bennett returned to the UK a happy man, with ten confirmed sales.

As usual Jim's racing season would be a financial struggle. Chevron supplied a chassis, with Choularton providing the engine. Graeme White, of Chevron, was keen to point out that it was not a factory entry. "It's not going to be a works effort in any way. I don't think Formula Atlantic can really stand a works team." Initially, the team was going to run under the famous Red Rose Racing name, but this was soon abandoned. With only enough funds for the first six meetings it was wisely decided to concentrate on the John Player championship, rather than contest the Southern Organs series as well.

First time out at Mallory Park and Jim put his B29 on pole by a second from Richard Morgan's example. In the race the positions were reversed, but second place was a solid start to the year. Round two at Brands saw Jim again battling with Morgan, in an eventful race for both men. Jim

was struggling with wet settings on a drying track and a troublesome engine. Despite this he was running ahead of Morgan until the protagonists touched going into Druids on lap 14. Morgan lost his nosecone while Jim spun. He quickly recovered, but was soon in trouble again. "Coming out of Bottom Bend, Crawford put the power on again – and the car turned right instead of going straight on, spinning him round three or four times. Fortunately there was nothing for him to hit and so he carried on, now having to make allowances for the fact that Morgan had altered his rear suspension slightly." Jim made short work of catching and passing the crippled Morgan, but by then Tony Brise was long gone in the Modus. He finished 37 seconds behind Brise, a portent of what was to come. After the meeting Jim was invited to Goodwood to test a Lotus 72 Formula One car, with Ronnie Peterson also in attendance.

The John Player series resumed at Snetterton in early April. After consultation the teams agreed to hold two heats of 30 laps each, with the overall result decided on aggregate times. This was to fill a gap in the programme due to not enough saloons appearing to merit two races. Brise claimed pole, with Jim second on the grid. During the warm-up laps it began to rain, which then turned to snow. After a delay the first heat got underway with everyone on wets (except the hapless Matt Spitzley, who had none). Brise led all the way, with Jim second and struggling with gearbox issues. Richard Morgan lost another nosecone on his way to third. In heat two Jim led initially, but on the fourth lap Brise got past and went on to win. Morgan also passed Jim, but the latter claimed second position overall once the times from both heats had been added together.

Before the next Atlantic round Jim was back in a Lotus 72 at Silverstone. Peter Warr also intended to be there, only to be involved in a collision with an army Land Rover en route. Warr was hospitalised, while his passenger (Lotus designer Ralph Bellamy) was uninjured. Jim was lucky to escape

Jim and Richard Morgan collide at Brands. **Boardman Family**

himself from a monumental accident during the test. It occurred at the dauntingly fast Abbey curve, as then-Lotus mechanic Keith Leighton recalls. "Jim got a puncture at 170mph. It let go and we didn't have safety beads in those days to keep it on the rim so the tyre came off and Jim was left with three wheels. The car dug in and came to rest upside down. I think he was the first guy to turn a 72 upside down!" Stephen Choularton was also present when the crash occurred. "Jim walked back to the pits with just the steering wheel in his hands and gave it to Colin [Chapman]. Colin went spare, but Peterson came in and told him the back wheel had dropped off. I think he actually told Colin the Lotus was a pile of crap." Peterson's reaction to the accident is recorded in the book *SuperSwede*, produced in conjunction with Alan Henry. "Ronnie's eyes bulged in amazement as he recounted the tale – Crawford appeared distinctly unruffled by the whole affair!"

Jim actually went off twice that day, something his friend Richard Jones remembers well. "I had been to see a potential sponsor in Birmingham, and headed for Silverstone on the way back. I knew Lotus were testing that day, although I didn't know if Jim was driving. I decided to stop at The Green Man pub nearby, and there was Jim! He was standing at the bar, staring into a pint and looking pretty sorry for himself. 'I've not had a very good day. I went off at Abbey, but the team had a spare car. So I went out in that, and crashed at the same place. I don't think Colin's very happy!'"

Despite this mishap Chapman soon chose to extend his option on Jim's services. He did this at Silverstone on the Friday morning of the International Trophy weekend,

a non-championship race set to see the debut of Jim in Formula One. Unfortunately, Jim almost immediately blotted his copybook by being rather too accommodating when allowing Patrick Depailler's Tyrrell past during practice. A dry line had appeared, but away from this the track was treacherously damp, and Jim's 72 slithered helplessly into the banking at Club corner, seriously damaging the chassis and ending his hopes of racing it on the Sunday. He did have rather more success in the supporting Atlantic race. Jim finished second to Tony Brise by three seconds after a close battle. Ted Wentz had applied considerable pressure to Brise before developing an engine misfire. The American remarked that Brise, "...was watching his mirrors like it was a sex film."

Ronnie Peterson was a driver Jim admired very much. Jim's friend Phil Smithies describes him as being "in awe" of Peterson. This admiration may well have had its roots in an incident at a previous Formula One event at Silverstone, where Choularton was competing in an Atlantic support race. He recalls the day:

"I nearly destroyed the field on the start-line in a massive shunt with Colin Vandervell, but during the F1 practice Jim was at Woodcote, which was a very fast long right-hander at the time. All the F1s came along and had a tentative lift just on the way in. It shifted the balance to the outer left front wheel and made them feel more confident. Ronnie came along and just went straight round with a touch of opposite lock. Jim came running back to me and dragged me to the corner to watch. We figured that if he could do it at 180mph we could do it at 150. When we went out in practice I had to actually hold my right knee down the first time through as

Waiting in the Silverstone pitlane during practice for the 1975 International Trophy. He would soon fall foul of the treacherous conditions. **Sue Deakin**

my brain wanted to force me to lift. I just locked my leg and in I went. Jim probably found it easier. Fantastic! The car just drifted across until the weight moved onto the left-hand wheels and round you went, with a touch of opposite lock. The only place I ever went faster was on the Mistral Straight at Ricard. I think it was two kilometres long and downhill. Incidentally, the dividend for bravery was nearly two seconds off our lap times and it allowed you to pass on the pit straight."

Jim remained fond of Peterson for the rest of his life. Peterson himself paid the sport's ultimate price in September 1978. A multiple pile-up at the start of that year's Italian Grand Prix left the Swede with broken legs. While his Lotus team-mate Mario Andretti went on to claim the World Championship that day Peterson was taken, conscious, to hospital. During the night complications set in and eventually claimed the life of the much-loved driver. The elation of his title success followed so closely by the news of his team-mate's death led Andretti to utter the poignant words, "Unhappily, motor racing is also this."

Later in April – while Lotus team leader Peterson was busy marrying his long-term partner Barbro – Jim was to be found enduring a difficult Atlantic weekend at Brands Hatch. He qualified poorly after various troubles in practice and finished the race fourth, with Brise inevitably winning again. Jim was still contending with serious handling issues during the following round at Silverstone. In desperation

the team fitted a Formula Two rear wing to the car. Despite this, nothing seemed to help the ill-handling Chevron. "Crawford was convinced that there was a magic tweak that was going to make his works development Chevron all come right, but until they found it, it was just a case of hopefully altering things and seeing the effect..."

Starting from the fourth row Jim found himself in a battle with Derek Cook, the former miner turned car salesman who would eventually build the successful DC Cook dealer group. Cook was driving Jim's championship winning B27 from the previous year. It turned out to be a meaningless fight as Jim was penalised one minute for jumping the start, leaving him dejected in 11th place. Brise once again claimed victory, and was now a fully-fledged Grand Prix driver. In between Atlantic commitments he drove for Graham Hill's team in the Spanish Grand Prix at Montjuich Park. He finished just outside the points on a difficult weekend which saw his team-mate Rolf Stommelen suffer a catastrophic wing failure. Pitched over a crash barrier Stommelen suffered multiple injuries, while his errant car killed five onlookers.

There was some light relief for Jim at Silverstone, when Geoff Wood offered him some practice laps in his Escort Supersaloon. "Dad knew Geoff Friswell and Jim through racing, and when he was getting too ill to drive offered both a chance to try out the car," remembers Wood's daughter, Felicity Brown. "Dad was very protective of his cars and

Jim dejectedly walks away after testing the Silverstone catch fencing during the GP-supporting Atlantic race. **Michael Pearson**

would only let someone who he knew well and trusted to drive them if he couldn't."

Determined to diagnose and eradicate the handling issue with his B29, Jim took team-mate Choularton's example round Oulton Park for comparison and easily lapped 1.5 seconds quicker than he could manage in his own car on the same day. Closer inspection revealed a fault with the monocoque itself, which was quickly put right. Back at Oulton with the repaired chassis, Jim was right on the pace at the end of May. In the Atlantic race he was running second to Brise, only for the engine to give up.

At Mallory in June Jim finally scored his first victory of the season, although Brise had retired from the race after breaking a half-shaft off the line. Jim had been unhappy with a Hart engine failure at the previous round and even tested a unit prepared by David Whitehurst before reverting to the Hart for the race. Brise was on pole next time out at Snetterton, but a gear selection problem saw him fluff the start. Richard Morgan took victory in the unique Wheatcroft 001, while Jim successfully fought off Brise to claim second.

Before the next Atlantic round at Silverstone events would conspire to hand Jim the opportunity to make his Formula One debut. Jacky Ickx had grown increasingly disillusioned with the failure of Lotus to provide him with competitive equipment. While Ronnie Peterson would drive whatever was given to him with minimal fuss, that was not in Ickx's nature. In the lead up to the British Grand Prix his patience finally ran out. Although he said publicly that he was stepping aside until the new Type 77 was available the veteran Belgian would never drive for the team again.

In the week before the Grand Prix Jim was summoned to Silverstone, along with Brian Henton. Both were given runs, Henton in a long wheelbase car, and Jim in the short wheelbase version. Jim posted the quicker time, but both would make their debuts that weekend. Brise would also be out in the Embassy Hill again, having finished sixth at the Swedish Grand Prix. This would prove to be the only world championship point the brilliant young Englishman scored in what should have been a glittering career.

Derek Bennett was delighted for Jim, and full of praise. "He's so much better than a lot of other people that fancy

their chances in a Formula One car. And what's more he's brave. He gets in a car and drives it. He doesn't mess about too much." Jim's call-up to a Lotus race seat came so late that he wasn't even listed as driving in the official programme. He was listed for the supporting Atlantic event however, and received a glowing write-up:

Another name to watch today is 27-year-old Jim Crawford, from Bolton in Lancashire, who drives a Chevron B29. Crawford had his first full season last year and put up some very impressive performances to win the Southern Organs championship and finish a close runner-up to John Nicholson in the John Player series. Despite his lack of experience Crawford was snapped up by Lotus last year to do some Formula 1 testing and he was actually entered to race in the International Trophy earlier this year in a Lotus

Jim on his Grand Prix debut at Silverstone. **Tim Marshall**

Following Atlantic sparring partner Dave Morgan's Surtees through the recently introduced Woodcote chicane. Jim had been the first driver to encounter it earlier that year. **Tim Marshall**

Jim looks helplessly towards the catch fencing as his Lotus slides off the damp circuit. Vittorio Brambilla can afford a quick glance at the scene as he passes in his March.
Michael Pearson (colour photo), Christian Wolf (black and white photos)

72. *Unfortunately a practice accident damaged the JPS too badly to race and Jim's Formula 1 career seems to have been temporarily put on ice. Consequently, beating Tony Brise must mean more to Jim Crawford than perhaps any driver in the race and for him to do so here in front of the Grand Prix teams would be an enormous morale booster for him. The Chevron seems to have suffered somewhat this year through being a larger car than the Modus and the Lola, but as Crawford's car is run by the works, Chevron designer Derek Bennett will be making sure that it has all the latest tweaks for today and Crawford should also start the race with a good chance of winning.*

The Atlantic race only brought disappointment. Jim – running with F2 suspension on his B29 – was eliminated after an altercation with Nick May at Becketts. Wentz took the win, while Jim mused on the difference between his Atlantic and Grand Prix cars. "It's a bit like towing the Queen Mary round after the F1."

In the Grand Prix itself Jim knew he had no chance of challenging the front-runners. Considering his recent history of accidents at Silverstone Jim understandably took a cautious approach to qualifying, lining up 25th. Even the great Peterson could only coax his 72 to 16th place. Brian Henton (also making his debut for Lotus) was sandwiched between his team-mates in 21st.

The race itself has passed into motor racing folklore. A sudden, isolated deluge on part of the circuit resulted in carnage, with cars spinning and crashing when they hit the water. By the time the monsoon arrived Jim's race was already run. He crashed out on lap 28 and was not classified.

For the next GP in Germany Jim was rested, with Northern Irishman John Watson piloting the only other Lotus alongside Peterson. Both cars were out by lap two. The Austrian GP saw Henton back in, but a crash in practice prevented him from starting. The race itself brought a much-needed boost of morale for the beleaguered team, with Peterson finishing fifth. It was, however, a tragic weekend for the sport. Popular American driver Mark Donohue crashed fatally during practice, with a marshal also losing his life.

Chapman was willing to give foreign talent a chance, which led to the team signing a young René Arnoux on a testing contract. Jim had raced against Arnoux in the autumn of 1974. After impressing Team Harper during a test drive at Silverstone they gave him a car for the non-championship round at Nogaro. David Gordon described the race in his book, *Chevron: The Derek Bennett Story*:

"Also making his Formula 2 debut that day, in an Elf, was Frenchman René Arnoux, who had been given an identical contract with Lotus. There was a general feeling that the two drivers were being played off against each other for the chance of greater things and it niggled Crawford when Arnoux beat him by one place at Nogaro." Nevertheless, fifth place on his Formula Two debut was a commendable

In action during the International F2 round at Silverstone at the end of August, where he so impressed engine builder Geoff Richardson. **Alan Cooper**

Jim has just passed Nick May for the lead, which he held to the flag at Mallory Park. **Alan Cox**

Lotus mechanic Clive Hicks wheels out Jim's Type 72 at Monza, while Arturo Merzario looks on, sporting his familiar cowboy hat. **Pietro Meller**

Jim pictured during practice, turning into the second Lesmo corner Following are Hans Stuck, Bob Evans and Roelof Wunderink. **Pietro Meller**

effort by Jim. He appeared in Formula Two again in 1975, retiring with a broken gearbox at Silverstone after holding an impressive fifth position in his B29, which carried ballast and was fitted with an ex-Le Mans BDG sports car engine. Engine builder Geoff Richardson said of Jim's drive, "If I'd known he was that good I'd have built him a proper engine."

At the end of August, Jim claimed another Atlantic victory, this time at Mallory Park's Fordsport Day. It kept him in contention for the title, but didn't come easily. After qualifying on pole Jim slipped back to third off the line, behind Australian Bob Muir's leading Birrane and Nick May. Muir had his day ruined by a combination of fuel feed issues and his cockpit fire extinguisher going off. With five laps to go Jim managed to pass May for the lead at Gerard's, and stayed there until the end.

Mallory was also the scene of a potentially serious, but ultimately comical, mishap which befell the team. Dave Taylor remembers it well. "We were at Mallory Park, I think it was with the Atlantic car. We were having our pictures taken, and the car was on its ramps on the trailer. The blinking winch jumped off the ratchet. The car rolled down the ramps and mowed everybody down!"

So to Monza, for the Italian Grand Prix, and Jim was back in favour. Practice was a fraught experience as he struggled to find the braking limits of the 72. As at Silverstone, Jim qualified 25th, but suffered a disastrous start to the race through no fault of his own. Vittorio Brambilla crept away in second gear (having lost first on the warm-up lap), causing much confusion behind him. Bob Evans in the BRM stalled. As Jim swerved to avoid Evans he was collected by Rolf Stommelen. Miraculously the car survived, albeit battered and with a shredded rear tyre. A slow lap and lengthy pitstop put paid to any chance of a decent result. Jim was eventually classified 13th, six laps behind Clay Regazzoni's winning Ferrari.

Although nobody knew it at the time, Jim's world championship Formula One career was over. Paul Carr

worked for Lotus at the time and was disappointed things didn't work out for his friend. "Jim had a raw edge to his driving, but quickly developed into a polished racing driver. Colin Chapman saw the real star in him and gave him that chance. Alas, it was very short-lived. Colin had his standards, but Jim was in the same mould as Ronnie Peterson – a real racer."

Years later Jim reflected on his taste of Formula One with typical honesty, speaking to Richard Williams in 1993. "It was a complete waste of time. I got into Formula One way too quickly. What I knew about racing cars, you could write on half a sheet of paper. When I started the British Grand Prix, that was only the 25th race I'd ever done. It was a joke."

Back in Atlantic, Jim's Mallory triumph meant he still stood a chance of claiming the John Player title as the series headed to the final round at Brands Hatch a week after Monza. In very wet conditions Jim did all he could, closing up on Gunnar Nilsson's ailing Chevron, only for his own engine to give up. With it went any chance of the title. Brise was content to be lapped twice on his way to being champion.

As 1975 drew to a close Jim's racing prospects were looking far bleaker than they had just 12 months previously. In the fickle business of motor racing today's rising star can quickly become yesterday's news. One upshot of his time with Lotus was a liberal supply of the title sponsor's product, unthinkable in today's Formula One. Ian Catt was a photographer for the team, but working in PR – including at Formula Atlantic rounds – at the time Jim was involved. "I also topped him up with cigarettes, as I was working at most of his UK races and the promotions team were given a supply of JPS to help 'grease the wheels of publicity.' All that was nearly 50 years ago, and what I would say is that it was always a pleasure to chat with Jim. He was very accommodating with regard to getting the JPS name over to any visitors/customers who would come to the circuits."

Chapter Five

What Now, Jim?

Jim had been harbouring hopes of a season in Formula Two, but the required sponsorship never materialised. Due to his usual lack of funds, Jim was left helping out around the Chevron works. This mainly consisted of driving one of the company's vans to various places around the country, collecting parts. Jim was always welcome at Chevron if he needed to make some money between races. The fact that he got along very well with Chevron founder Derek Bennett didn't surprise Kevin Hodgkinson. "Jim and Derek were very much alike, in that they were both introverted. To give an example, I joined Chevron in 1968. I'd only been there four weeks and was busy working on a car with another guy. I said to him, 'When's this Derek Bennett character going to show up?' He replied shyly, 'Well actually, that's me.' Derek kept a very low profile, and Jim was the same."

Chevron was very much a small operation taking on the big boys. Richard Sproston remembers the early days of the company. "I used to hang around the front door. Derek Bennett would be fabricating something, and Brian Redman would go and get fish and chips for everyone." Dave Taylor worked there at the time. "There was a café at the end of Chorley Old Road called The Copper Kettle. I've been in there with Count Rudy Van der Straten, who owned Stella Artois. He'd be eating beans on toast with Derek!"

Jim was a sporadic competitor in the Shellsport International Series, which featured an eclectic mix of machinery. He piloted a Chevron B29 with a 1.6 litre Ford BDA. Sponsorship came from *Coin News*, a magazine for numismatists. Up against big banger Formula 5000s he stood no chance of overall victory. After missing the first two rounds Jim appeared at Oulton Park in mid-April, finishing a creditable fifth albeit one lap down. The winner was Damien Magee in a March 751, a pukka F1 car. Just three days later a misfire put him out at Brands Hatch. Following a non-start at Thruxton Jim didn't appear again, his solitary fifth place giving him 27th place

Jim looks far from happy with his lot in this 1976 portrait. **Alan Cox**

in the final standings.

Jim also popped up in a Renault 5 at Mallory Park, convincingly beating the series regulars. "Neil McGrath made his customary fast start in the Renault 5 race to lead until half distance, but former Grand Prix driver Jim Crawford nipped past and pulled away. What a waste of talent!" Jim even appeared on the entry list for the 1977 Le Mans 24 Hours, listed among the drivers of a Chevron B31 for Chandler Ibec International – Team Lloyds. Jim never did drive in the French classic, something which Le Mans veteran Richard Jones thinks was a missed opportunity. "Jim would have been fantastic at Le Mans. He would have known how to manage that race."

Chris Kellett experienced Jim's night driving first hand, as a passenger in his Alfa Romeo on the notorious Scout Road near Bolton. It is an experience which remains etched in his memory. "We had been for a pint at the Blundell Arms, and we headed back over Scout Road. I don't know why he went that way. Well, I do. Because he was crackers! You head downwards to a quarry, and there's a 100-foot drop. The road turns ninety degrees left. I remember approaching that corner and the alternator went down on the car, so all the lights went out. I said, 'Jim, don't you think you should back off?' He said, 'It's only like being int' dark at Le Mans, i'nt it? Just count before you get t' corner and hit the anchors.' Next thing, the lights came on and all I could see was an armco barrier about 100 feet in front of us, and we were flat in fifth. He had commitment!"

Scout Road was also the setting for perhaps Jim's most comprehensive demolition of a road car. Paddy Atkinson was with him at their friend John Horrock's house, where a party was in full swing. "Jim and myself were sitting having a drink and catching up," remembers Atkinson. "John [Horrocks] suddenly said to Jim, 'It's snowing!' He had a new Saab that he thought Jim should take for a spin, as he'd fitted studded tyres for the winter. Jim eventually relented after some persuasion and the two of us headed out to have

An atmospheric paddock shot by Geoff Werran. Jim appears to be chatting to Chevron founder Derek Bennett (leaning against the SDC transporter), while his car is worked on. Jim and Derek got on famously. **Geoff Werran**

Jim's final appearance of 1976 was behind the wheel of a Chevron B34, at the Brands Hatch James Hunt Victory Meeting in November. Although his career was in the doldrums, Jim's driving remained as committed as ever. **Alan Cooper**

some fun. Jim started doing pirouettes on the street outside, but eventually got bored of that. 'Enough snow, where's the ice?' So, we headed towards Belmont, over Scout Road. Jim clipped the inside of a corner and just had time to say 'Oh shit!' before the car buried itself in a wall. I looked across but there was no sign of Jim, but then I heard giggling coming from the back seat. The driver's seat mounting had broken, and Jim was just lying there in hysterics. We climbed out, unsure of what to do. Jim said, 'We better not stand around here, but we better not go back to the party either!' We eventually made it to a phone and gave John a ring. He asked Jim where the car was. 'On Scout Road.' 'Someone might nick it.' 'No, they won't!' Jim assured him."

Jim Crawford was a name well known around Bolton by this time. Kellett was at Chevron one night when Jim and a friend took a couple of road cars for a high-speed dash around the city. The police briefly attempted a pursuit, but realising the futility of it, made their way to the factory to await their prey. Unable to find the number one suspect, an officer remarked to those present, "This reeks of Crawford!"

One of Chevron's customers was Walter Frey, the head of Toyota Switzerland and gentleman racing driver. His team was run by Freddy Kessler and, when they took delivery of a new Formula Three car, they also requested some help with setting it up due to their inexperience with such a machine. With Jim not up to much he was dispatched to Switzerland, where he met up with old friend Mike Peers. The latter was enjoying a long vacation with his sister after finishing university. Peers would quickly become a significant figure in Jim's life, but at the time they were more interested in having fun, as Peers remembers. "Jim had never driven a Formula Three car and he made

me drive it to start with. It was great fun, tearing round and round this huge motor compound."

Jim and Mike stayed just outside Zurich, where the pair shared a hotel room. Despite being there for some considerable time Jim didn't make any great effort to learn the language. "The only word he ever learned was *blumenkohl*, which means cauliflower. He liked cauliflower. Jim was the most non-European man you could wish to meet. He drank lager, disliked most foreign cuisine and communicated with the locals using hand gestures."

During 1977 Peers effectively became the road manager for Kessler's team. Kessler was an amateur driver, who enjoyed racing but knew his limitations. Peers remembers an episode before a race at Brands Hatch. "It was raining and Freddy said to me, 'I've decided, Michael, that I won't be racing today.'" The team received some factory support from Chevron and had a reasonably successful year. If Kessler knew his limitations on the track, however, on the public road it was a different story. He had the alarming habit of driving extremely quickly with his pet dachshund sitting on his lap. On the way back from a test at Dijon he lost control and slammed into a bridge. Jim and Mike were also in the car, all three miraculously walking away. Mike noted that, "the only panel that wasn't damaged was the boot lid."

This accident aside, Jim and Mike enjoyed a somewhat idyllic life in Switzerland. In May, with a few days off, Frey handed them a considerable wad of money and the keys to a Mini Innocenti, with instructions to take a break. Requiring no further encouragement, the pair were soon in the south of France, taking in the Monaco Grand Prix. Peers remembers the trip well. "We were always

> Jim was the most non-European man you could hope to meet

Ready for the start at his beloved Oulton Park in the Coin News Chevron. Note the rather natty footwear on the extreme right of the picture. **Boardman Family**

racing people. On the drive down we always managed to find someone who wanted to race us."

On another trip Jim found himself in a tiny Swiss village, where the team was running a local driver in a hillclimb. He soon found the nearest bar, with Mike in tow. "We ended up at a barn dance. People were practising their English on us. It was full of farmers, drinking furiously and reminiscent of the Wild West. Next thing, a chair came over. We just stood there as all hell broke loose, with everyone fighting around us."

The two Brits in Switzerland eventually became three, when Tony Dron joined them as part of an ill-fated project to develop a Triumph Dolomite Sprint for racing. The car's debut would be at the Nürburgring. Dron knew the circuit well, unlike Jim. With Peers also onboard the trio hammered around the 14-mile track daily, paying their five deutschmarks for each lap. The vehicle they had for the purpose is described by Peers as, "probably the most unsuitable car you could imagine, an Austin Princess. It was like a *Top Gear* challenge, and by then end of it we had completely destroyed the thing." Each day's schedule

usually consisted of lunch in a nice restaurant at Adenau Bridge, accompanied by some wine, followed by several high-speed laps.

Jim would drive the Dolomite on just one occasion in the European Touring Car Championship (ETCC), at Zandvoort in Holland, entered alongside Alec Poole and Paul Keller. The result was a DNF, and another intended entry at Zolder a few weeks later (partnering Tony Dron) failed to materialise. Near the end of the 1977 season Jim made his Formula Three debut at Mallory Park, in a one-off appearance driving Thorkild Thyrring's Chevron. He qualified 16th, but moved up to eighth by the end of the race.

For 1978 the intrepid duo returned to the UK to tackle domestic Formula Three properly with a Chevron B43 funded by Peers Construction. Based in Bolton, Mike Peers Racing would eventually operate from the premises of Halbro, a printing company owned by Jim's great friend, Rob Moores. Faith in his ability and loyalty from his entrants was to become a feature of Jim's career. Peers was one of those who had total belief in his friend. "I created

Mike Peers Racing to look after Jim." The team's prospected expenditure for the season was outlined in the sponsorship proposals sent out to various companies:

1 Chevron B43 – £9800
1 Toyota engine (Novamotor) – £5000
8 Spare wheels – £500
1 Spare nose cone – £125
3 Nose splitters – £120
General spares – £1500
General equipment – £500
1 Ford transporter (on loan) – £2000
TOTAL VALUE OF ASSETS – £19,545

Sunday, March 12th 1978 was a black day for motor racing in general and Chevron in particular. Derek Bennett's lifelong love of aviation had led him to become an avid hang glider. Jim had accompanied Bennett on at least one occasion to Winter Hill, near Belmont village just outside of Bolton. Neil Edwards was also there to assist, as David Gordon recalls in *Chevron: The Derek Bennett Story*:

"Eventually they all ended up running down the hill together, Derek in the harness and Jim and Neil holding a wing-tip each. Finally his feet came a few feet off the ground and he 'flew' for a couple of hundred yards. 'All you could hear was "Yeeeaaaahhh!"', Crawford recalls. 'I'd never heard anything like it in my life!' They were just as bemused a couple of minutes later when the normally sullen Derek Bennett reappeared, walking back up towards them, beaming from ear to ear and laughing uproariously."

On March 12th Bennett's luck ran out. While competing in a competition at Lobden Moor he lost control of his hang glider and fell to earth from a height of approximately 50 feet. He was transported to hospital in Rochdale with serious head injuries. Bennett clung on for over a week, before finally succumbing on March 22nd, aged just 44. Mike Peers is another person with fond memories of the late Chevron founder. "Some American guys came to buy Chevrons. When they arrived Derek was sweeping up outside in a brown shop coat. He never let on who he was, just sent them straight upstairs to see Dave Wilson." Dave Taylor also remembers his boss's innate need to avoid unwanted attention. "Derek was a very, very shy guy. He was like the Scarlet Pimpernel. He'd just drift away from a group conversation, because he was that shy."

A few days after Bennett's death Jim was fortunate to escape from a horrific looking accident during the Easter meeting at Thruxton. After losing control on the fast back part of the track his Chevron cartwheeled to destruction. Jim climbed from the wreckage, casually picked up the headrest which had flown off and tossed it into the cockpit. Peers remembers the weekend vividly. "We were still preparing the car at Chevron on the Friday. Jim qualified quite well and was running near the front in the race. He disappeared off the lap chart but we had no idea what had happened. Next thing we know he appears on foot in the pitlane with mud all down one side of his overalls. I asked him, 'Where the fuck have you been? In a field?' 'Eh, yeah, and wait till you see the car!'" The spectacular crash would be replayed countless times in living rooms throughout the land, as it featured in the opening credits to ITV's *World of Sport*.

Jim soon had a new Chevron B43 to drive but, overall, the 1978 season was one to forget. It had started well enough, at Silverstone in March. In qualifying Jim was the quickest Chevron and fourth fastest overall, but in the race he spun into retirement. He was now driving the ex-Thyrring car permanently. That was the plan anyway, until the accident at Thruxton.

Silverstone and Thruxton set the tone for the year. In the end the team missed several rounds, and the season eventually petered out altogether. The budget didn't stretch to competing at Monaco in May, a circuit Jim would never get the chance to race at. He finished 15th equal in the final standings of the the BP Super Visco F3 Championship,

The hotel where Jim and Mike Peers resided while in Switzerland, and a copy of the menu Jim kept, featuring the famous blumenkohl. **Boardman Family**

Despite his best efforts Jim had neither the budget or the equipment to win. **Alan Cox**

A promotional photo ahead of the 1978 F3 season. Jim is in the car, as Mike Peers crouches alongside with clipboard, while an attractive assistant perches on the bodywork. **Mike Peers**

Jim waits in the Oulton Park pitlane. He went on to score his best result of the 1978 season, third. **Boardman Family**

tied with Siegfried Stohr, who was also in a B43. In the Vandervell series Jim was 21st equal, with future Formula One drivers Andrea de Cesaris and Teo Fabi. The Toyota GB F3 Award points table ended with Jim in fifth place, while Derek Warwick was a runaway winner.

The Mallory Park round in May had provided a rare highlight, when he was joint quickest with Piquet in wet practice and finished fifth in the race. On home ground at Oulton Park, Jim was also competitive, and able to remind people of his talent. In April he finished third, and was fourth when the F3 cars returned in May. Apart from those occasions there wasn't much to celebrate. A trip to Paul Ricard for a BP round in July started well enough, with Jim qualifying tenth, but his car broke down on the warm-up lap. Jim's efforts only received a fleeting mention in the *Autosport* seasonal survey. "Chevron's interest in England, strangely, was almost zero with only former employees Jim Crawford and Barry Green showing any pace in the latest B43 model..."

Jim and the B43 also made a few late season appearances in the European Formula Three championship. He raced at Knutstorp and Karlskoga in Sweden on consecutive weekends in August. At Knutstorp Jim finished seventh in his heat, but collided with Jan Ridell in the final, putting both drivers out. He was fourth in his heat at Karlskoga a week later, but dropped to 12th in the final. In the final round of the year, at Valellunga in October, Jim qualified 24th and finished 16th.

Despite being a frustrating year on the track, away from it Jim was his usual fun-loving self. Socialising was a major part of his life, as Peers remembers. "No-one trained back then. Our friend Dave Gill kept piranha. They hated Saturday nights. We'd all come back drunk and have a competition to see who could keep

We used to race up and down Kirkstone Pass, stopping for scampi at the top

their hand in the tank the longest!" An addition to their group was an American who they were helping as he tried his hand at European racing. "He was a good-looking guy, with wealthy parents, but a crap driver." Jim also continued to indulge his passion for sailing, particularly on Lake Windermere. The sinuous country lanes of the Lake District gave him plenty of opportunity to hone his driving skills further, with Peers for company. "We used to race up and down Kirkstone Pass, stopping for scampi at the top."

Jim also kept up to date with goings-on in the sailing world, and visited the Boat Show that year with friends Rob Moores and Richard Cort, as the latter well remembers. "We drove down in my Morris Ital, with plans to buy a Halberg-Rassy." Their plans hit a major hitch when they had the misfortune to bump into some legendary racers, who were also legendary drinkers. Cort again – "We met Tony Lanfranchi, Barrie Williams and Gerry Marshall, and got blitzed on Guinness. Then we decided we'd start drinking port. A girl in a bar – I remember she had a cleaning company – took pity on us and let us stay. Jim was going to drive home!"

Chapter Six

Back on Track

After the disappointment of his Formula Three season Jim returned to Formula Atlantic in 1979, again driving for Mike Peers. Rumours at the end of 1978 had Jim spearheading a six-car F3 team for Toyota Switzerland, with sidecar ace Rolf Biland among the other drivers. This ultimately failed to materialise. Sponsorship for the Atlantic assault included backing from Plygrange, a company relatively new to the racing scene but one which would become synonymous with Jim's career.

The Plygrange organisation comprised a number of businesses specialising in building work, heating systems and several other areas. The racing connection came about in 1977, when Plygrange started sponsoring company MD Ken Donaldson-Gough's brother Gerry, who raced a modified Mini with considerable success. Plygrange was a family affair. Ken Gough's wife Judith also purchased a Chevron B19 for Vin Malkie to drive in Libre and HSCC (Historic Sports Car Club) events. Plygrange's first step into single-seater racing was a tentative one. They supported Jim in the early rounds of the Hitachi Formula Atlantic series, but when Econopallet appeared with sponsorship money they withdrew for the time being.

The Formula Atlantic series Jim returned to was a shadow of the one he'd made his name in during 1974 and 1975. There had been no series at all in 1977 and 1978. Jim's stiffest competition would come from Ray Mallock in his Ralt RT1, a modified Formula Two car. The schedule included a 'Triple Crown', consisting of three rounds, one each in England (Donington Park), Scotland (Ingliston) and Ireland (Mondello Park). An exclusive pre-season Atlantic test was also held at Paul Ricard.

The season opened at a wet and miserable Mallory Park, a meeting Jim was absent from. Victory went to Alo Lawlor in a Lola. Andrew Jeffrey's Chevron was the only other car to finish on the same lap. The Plygrange team made its debut

Iain Nicolson captured Jim's only racing appearance in his homeland when he raced at Ingliston in 1979. A relaxed atmosphere in the paddock, and at speed on his way to victory around the tight, challenging circuit. **Iain Nicolson**

at Thruxton on April Fool's Day, but it was a disappointing weekend with Jim only managing a seventh-place finish. He had battled with Mallock for the lead until his engine went on to three cylinders. A week is a long time in racing, however, and seven days later Jim was right on the pace at Silverstone. He finished second to a dominant Mallock, but only after surviving a final lap scare. At Woodcote, Alo Lawler tried desperately to nick the position, only to slide off into the catch fencing.

From Silverstone it was on to Brands Hatch for the non-championship Race of Champions meeting. Jim qualified fifth on a combined F2/Atlantic grid, but was punted off on the second lap, while victory went to fellow Scot Norman Dickson in his Hart engined March. The Atlantics were back at Brands Hatch a fortnight later and Jim had a more fruitful weekend, qualifying and finishing second. It was the same story next time out at Mallory Park, as Jim once again had to cede victory to Mallock. Mallock's performances were rewarded with a drive in the Aurora series, piloting a Formula One Surtees for four rounds. It was an initiative which had already benefited Tiff Needell earlier in the season. In the event, it was an unmitigated disaster. Mallock drove one round with no testing beforehand, and then the car failed to arrive for the next one.

At Silverstone in June, Jim finished third, despite serious braking and rear-end stability problems. At the end of the month the Atlantic brigade descended on Oulton Park, Jim's favourite stomping ground. Although he could only record the second quickest time in qualifying Jim ran away with the race, beating Paul Smith's March by 15 seconds. By this stage of the season it was clear that Mallock, Smith and Crawford were the class of the field.

After finishing second to Mallock at Snetterton, Jim won the Triple Crown Atlantic race at Donington, once again from Smith. Although a start crash took out Mallock, Lawler and others the two leaders had been over a second quicker than anyone in practice. On July 22nd Jim found himself racing on Scottish soil for the first and only time in his career. The circuit was Ingliston, located next to Edinburgh airport. It was a perfect weekend, with Jim taking pole position and victory, although Mallock and Smith were notable absentees from the meeting.

Mallock and Smith were back again at Mallory Park, but neither could beat Jim, who won again, this time by half a minute. After a lacklustre fifth place at Silverstone Jim maintained his 100 percent winning record around Oulton Park before rounding off the year with a second place at Brands Hatch behind Mallock's new Ralt RT4. Jim's five victories earned him second place overall in the final standings, 32 points behind champion Mallock.

Despite his up and down career since the disappointment of Formula One with Lotus, Jim remained a highly respected driver. Fellow Northerner and long-time entrant Rodney Dodson admired his ability to remain grounded, even when he was winning regularly:

"While other drivers were partying and jet setting Jim would drive his standard yellow Ford Escort to the Little Lever Working Men's Club on Wednesday and Friday nights, providing he was not racing. He regarded himself as a jobbing racing driver, with no pretentious ideals. However, he was very underrated and could drive any formula with great speed and bravery, but perhaps lacked a little ambition." Dick Carpenter, promotions manager for Hitachi UK, was full of praise. "1979 was our first season in

Jim regarded himself as a jobbing racing driver, with no pretentious ideals

single-seater racing and, to have drivers with the capability that Jim Crawford has shown, helped to make our championship such a success. It has shown that Jim Crawford, who has competed against some very well-known drivers, has the potential to win Grand Prix races. We will be very sorry to lose him." By the end of the 1979 season, Jim received the Dish of the Year award, a title bestowed upon the favourite driver chosen by lady marshals at Silverstone.

Jim was initially to be backed by Econopallet again for the 1980 season, but the deal collapsed when the company went into liquidation. It was at this point that Plygrange re-entered the fray. Mike Peers had spent the close season changing the B42 to B45 Formula Two specification. He then proposed entering the

Celebrating victory at Oulton Park in September. **Alan Cox**

was already two years old when the season started. Despite this, the 1980 season would turn out to be arguably the greatest of his career.

The Aurora season opened on April 4th at Oulton Park. Qualifying saw Jim finish seventh fastest, just behind the leading F2 of Mather. Given the clutch and ignition problems he had to deal with Jim must have been relatively content. He was also suffering handling trouble, as related to *Autosport*. "It's totally unmanageable on the new tyres, but plenty spectacular. Anyway, it might even rain tomorrow – I'll love that – so it's no use worrying."

It didn't rain, but Jim held his own in the dry to finish fourth after a spirited duel with Mather. The three cars ahead of Jim were all F1s, with the race victory going to Guy Edwards in an Arrows.

Aurora AFX championship to Ken Gough, who was quick to sign up. With only one full time mechanic (John Connel) it may have looked on paper like a shoestring affair, but the Plygrange team quickly established themselves as models of flawless preparation and professionalism. Jim was looking forward to a new challenge. "I don't see much future in Atlantic, so we'll have a bash at Aurora."

The Aurora series was a British championship for Formula One cars, but there was also a Formula Two class which bolstered the grid. The series sponsor, Aurora, manufactured scale model slot racing cars. The category had replaced Group 8 (previously Formula 5000) in 1978 and provided an ideal home for second-hand F1 machinery. Some of the machinery was very recent indeed. During 1980 Emilio de Villota and Eliseo Salazar both appeared in Williams FW07s. While they were competing for the Aurora title Alan Jones was taking a version of the same car to the Formula One World Championship.

In the F2 category Jim faced competition from, amongst others, fellow Brits Brian Robinson (Chevron B38 and B42) and Kim Mather (March 802). Jim's converted Atlantic car

For Jim it was a bittersweet success. Near the end a broken valve spring forced him to slow and tour around to the chequered flag. The next round was at Brands Hatch just two days later, which gave Plygrange no chance to fix the engine. Jim would have to sit that one out.

A fortnight later the B45 was sorted and ready for round three at Silverstone. The Northamptonshire circuit's long straights were hardly ideal territory for the Chevron, but Jim managed tenth on the grid, once again just behind Mather. The two became embroiled in another frantic battle, regularly lowering the F2 lap record throughout the race. Jim eventually gained the upper hand and pulled away to finish sixth, on the same lap as three of the F1 machines in front of him. It was enough to earn him the Driver of the Day award. Before the next Aurora round at Mallory Park, Jim headed for Brands Hatch to share a Colt Mirage GLX with his friend, Barrie Williams, in a 500km race. The happy duo qualified 15th, only for the engine to fail in the race itself.

It was then on to Mallory, and it would prove to be a fraught weekend for Jim and the Plygrange team. By now the B45 was running on Goodyear tyres and Jim was

The visually appealing Plygrange livery stood out in the Aurora field. **Alan Cooper**

struggling to get them to work, as he told *Autosport*. "'When you can get them to slide, and not grip, they work very well... but they suddenly snatch away when more wing is put on to make them stick... We should be a second quicker, and that would give the F1 drivers something to worry about', grinned the Dunfermline-born man."

Despite the problems Jim still qualified fastest of the F2s, ahead of Mather and Warren Booth. In the race itself Jim had to contend with serious brake trouble in addition to his handling woes. Mather had comfortably led the F2 class until a clutch failure put him out. Jim inherited the lead but his 30 second gap to Booth's Chevron B48 began to rapidly evaporate as his brake issues got worse. "By pumping everywhere I could occasionally get the right front to work a little." Despite Booth's best efforts Jim held on to take third place overall and first in the F2 class by the matter of a few feet.

The next two rounds did nothing to help Jim's points tally. A 13th at Thruxton was followed by a trip to Monza. The team must have wondered why they bothered after distributor failure put Jim out. Marcus Pye was reporting on the race at Monza and remembers the weekend well. "Jim, and John Connel, were great, great fun. We were all staying at the same hotel. They ended up back in my room the night before the race, where they completely emptied my mini bar. Then they went downstairs to the hotel bar, which was just closing but still open for residents. They proceeded to buy a bottle of Scotch at nip prices, and managed to stick it on someone else's room! They were really proud of that. Even though they polished it off it didn't stop Jim racing really convincingly the following day."

With a month in between Thruxton and Monza the Plygrange team decided to try their hand at European Formula Two, a prestigious and highly competitive championship at the time. Jim's archaic B45 must have drawn some curious glances from Europe's elite racing teams when it arrived in the Silverstone paddock, but

anyone laughing then certainly wouldn't have been come the end of the weekend. In a drive which would live long in the memory of anyone who witnessed it Jim simply thrashed the little Chevron around Silverstone's high-speed turns. The main target of Jim's attention on race day was the German Manfred Winkelhock in his March 802, the difference in age between the two cars obvious to even the most casual onlooker. Winkelhock simply could not shake off the Plygrange machine, and although Jim's day eventually ended in an engine failure he had made a very big statement. The talent was all still there.

Back to Aurora business, where Mallory and Snetterton both yielded fourth place finishes. A fine sixth at Brands on the Grand Prix circuit came before another DNF at Thruxton. Mather would prove to be a threat all season to Jim and the Plygrange team. He, too, had his struggles that year. "Jack Kelly bought a March 802 for me, which was £15,000. My house was insurance against it. I had built it for £7000 and it was worth £16,000 to £17,000. During my first test with it at Oulton Park the thing swapped ends going up Clay Hill. We struggled with the tyres. We would do three laps during practice, come in, and then do another 10 to 15 laps. We couldn't match our times though. It took us three or four races to realise that the tyres were shite. You had to run them with higher pressures. Jim and his team had sussed this out well before us." The March 802 Mather campaigned was designed as a ground-effect car, but had to run without it in Aurora. "I thought I was going to get my big break that year, but the car had no grip without the ground effects, and the geometry didn't work."

The rain, which Jim had yearned for at the opening round at Oulton Park finally arrived during the penultimate race of the Aurora season in September at the same track. It would prove to be a memorable day in the life of Jim, the Plygrange team and anyone who was there to witness it.

Qualifying at Oulton Park contained no hint of what was to transpire on race day. As usual, the F1 cars dominated

Battling hard to stay ahead of Kim Mather during the opening Aurora round at Oulton Park. **Alan Cox**

Running ahead of the much newer Ralts driven by Rad Dougall (9) and future F1 world champion Nigel Mansell (34). **Alejandro de Brito**

Jim harrying Manfred Winkelhock at Silverstone. **Alejandro de Brito**

Seeking shelter from the rain at Oulton Park, along with Aurora rival Kim Mather. Fellow Chevron driver Warren Booth, between them, appears to be holding court. **Peter McFadyen**

proceedings. Salazar claimed pole in his Williams, with champion elect de Villota alongside in his similar FW07B. Edwards qualified third, but the fact he was on the grid at all was a minor miracle. Having comprehensively damaged his Arrows in a huge practice shunt his team worked flat out to rebuild the car. He repaid them by qualifying third then crashing again during the warm-up on race day morning. Once again his loyal mechanics set to work and ensured he took the start. Behind Edwards was Musetti in his Bennett F5B, which was actually a rebadged Fittipaldi F1 car. Jim was a frustrated sixth on the grid and not even the fastest F2 runner, for between Musetti and himself was Mather's March.

Jim's mood improved considerably on race day as Oulton Park suffered a deluge. By the time of the Aurora event, however, the rain appeared long gone and it was slicks all round. The order remained the same at the start, apart from Edwards

> In the wet conditions he had been praying for all year he annihilated the opposition

sneaking ahead of de Villota. Salazar's title hopes vanished on lap 15 when he had to retire with brake trouble. His retirement was good news for Jim. While crawling back to the pits Salazar inadvertently forced Musetti off the circuit and the Plygrange Chevron nipped past. A short time later de Villota relieved Edwards of the race lead and pulled away.

The rain returned, quickly developing into a downpour. De Villota and Mather pitted for wets, leaving Edwards leading the race from Jim. The Plygrange team knew they would have to bring Jim in for wets, but a shortage of personnel led to an extraordinary turn of events, as Mike Peers remembers. "Jim was well liked, and so were the team. We were always underdogs but doing a good job. With Jim looking like he could win the race some of the F1 guys came down and helped us change tyres! It was always good fun in Aurora. We raced hard, but would meet up with the other teams in the bar after."

Jim raises his arm as he crosses the line to take an extraordinary outright win against F1 opposition. **Peter McFadyen**

With the circuit awash and Jim at one with the Chevron, he quickly closed in on de Villota's Williams and brushed past. De Villota wouldn't finish, after a contentious collision with Warren Booth's Chevron B48. Jim pulled out a huge lead and looked set for victory with less than five laps to go. Jim described what happened next. "The engine suddenly cut out – silence – and that five grand seemed a long way away."

After what must have seemed an interminable delay the engine fired again, and Jim was on his way. He crossed the line 35 seconds ahead of Mather, with Musetti third. It was a fairytale result, and the only time in the history of the Aurora series that an F2 car would score an outright race win. For Plygrange Jim's victory couldn't have happened at a better place. The team had 260 guests on hand to witness it. Marcus Pye summed up Jim's achievement in the introduction to his *Autosport* report. "Jim Crawford scored the most popular victory of the entire Aurora AFX championship at Oulton Park on Saturday when, in the wet conditions he had been praying for all year,

he annihilated the opposition... ample justification of our remark earlier in the season that Jim has more flair than everyone else in the championship."

Bob Fernley was at Oulton Park that day and Jim's performance left a lasting impression on him. Fernley campaigned a Chevron in some Libre events, but also ran AMCO. "Bobby Howlings and I were partners in AMCO Motors, which specialised in buying and selling Formula One cars, and was probably the first company to recognise modern Formula One cars as being collectable." Fernley would soon come to play a pivotal role in Jim's career.

Jim's 1980 season petered out with an eighth place at Silverstone, but nevertheless he finished the year fourth overall in the standings and easily the best F2 runner. Marcus Pye was impressed by Jim's achievements in the old Chevron. "He was wringing some incredible times from it. Jim and John were both wonderful mechanics of course. It was very rare for just a driver and mechanic to turn up and be so successful."

Chapter Seven

European Swansong

Jim had serious backing for 1981, and started the season with high hopes.
Boardman Family

In 1981 saw Plygrange took the ambitious and expensive step up to European Formula Two. A pre-season newspaper feature on the single-car team gave its forecasted budget for the season as £245,250. Jim would pilot a Hart-powered Toleman TG280 (an ex-works car), and was optimistic about his chances. First time out at Silverstone seemed to justify Jim's optimism as he finished fourth on a wet track, despite a very late tyre change as the pitlane closed. In the next race at Hockenheim he was just outside the points in seventh, before consecutive DNFs at Thruxton (engine) and the Nürburgring (suspension). Despite these setbacks Jim remained upbeat. "It's a hell of a responsibility... But I believe the car is right now for winning, I'm backed by a dedicated, professional team and I feel I'm at the peak of my career."

Unfortunately, the season quickly descended into a hugely frustrating experience. Unreliability and uncompetitive tyres proved to be insurmountable obstacles. Pirelli (supplying the vast majority of the field) soon found themselves upstaged by Bridgestone, and unable to supply its latest developments to all but a few. Jim wasn't among the chosen ones. The team eventually switched to M&H rubber. At Vallelunga in May, Jim at least finished the race, but he was ninth and a full two laps behind Eje Elgh's winning Maurer. Ironically, although a German owned team, the Maurers were built at the old Chevron works in Bolton, by several former Chevron staff.

Mugello in Tuscany was the next stop. The top 12 cars finished on the lead lap, with Jim 11th behind the ill-fated young Italian driver, Riccardo Paletti, who would die following a startline shunt at the Canadian Grand Prix the following year. From Mugello the Plygrange team travelled to the sinuous Pau street circuit in southern France. Despite his best efforts, Jim finished the day in tenth, last car running.

Round nine at Spa brought a rare highlight in an otherwise dismal season. After qualifying tenth Jim was quickest of all in morning warm-up. The race start was delayed by rain but, by the time the field pulled away,

In action at the Nürburgring, negotiating the famous Karussell. **Michael Pearson**

An unusual view of Jim in the Plygrange Toleman.
Chris Walker, kartpix.net

*Jim captured in the process of obliterating
the Croft lap record. **Tony Todd***

everyone was on slicks. The rain returned briefly just after
half distance, by which time Jim was struggling with a
broken rear wing. For much of the race he was involved in
close battles, eventually crossing the line sixth. It would
prove to be his second and last points finish of the year,
although he was all set for one at Misano until a fuel pick-up
issue intervened. Despite the disappointing results there
could be no doubting Jim's commitment to the cause. "With
no rear end downforce to speak of, Jim was entertaining
the crowds all round the circuit with oversteer slides and
they gave him an ovation at the end. If he starts to make his
own wings to match his other work, he's got a consistent
championship points challenger." Away from the track,
Jim did his best to take his mind off his racing troubles.
Stuart Dent was working for the Docking Spitzley team
that year, and met Jim at Spa. "Jim and I managed to get a
ridiculously favourable exchange rate from our hosts, and
then persuaded them to let us serve ourselves at the bar
after they'd gone to bed. Silly buggers!"

With Geoff Lees having wrapped up the title at Misano
the final round in Sweden was something of an anti-climax.
After qualifying tenth in freezing conditions Jim tangled
with fellow Brit Mike Thackwell on the opening lap, from

which both men's cars emerged unscathed. Jim was heading
for a seventh-place finish, only to be mugged by a whole
group of drivers shortly before the end. He crossed the line
a despondent tenth. All in all, 1981 had been a costly failure.
Jim wasn't one to wallow in self-pity, however, as Stuart
Dent again remembers. "The post-race evening involved
food fights and then hire car races, in reverse and on wet
cobblestones, between Plygrange, Docking Spitzley, March
and Maurer!"

Despite now regularly travelling to race in mainland
Europe Jim still enjoyed getting home and catching up
with old friends. He was never what could be described as
generous at the bar, but Chris Kellett never held anything
against him. "Jim never carried any money, typical
Scotsman! [laughs]. He was just a very, very friendly and
approachable man. It didn't matter what you were talking
about, he was so knowledgeable. He didn't come across that
way though. He was quick at arithmetic. I think he got that
from playing darts and dominoes in pubs!"

One source of light relief during that trying year was
provided by Formula Libre races back in England. On a free
weekend Jim liked nothing better than to turn up with his
Toleman and blitz the outright lap record. The most notable

Jim led easily until he encountered Arnold Glass. **Steve Jones**

example of this came at the Croft Autodrome in North Yorkshire, where fans were treated to a truly spectacular lap, Jim setting a new record which will never be beaten as the layout no longer exists. Mike Peers failed to see the point of it all. "There was no upside to it. He was expected to win and beat the lap record. He once spun off at Aintree and everyone cheered!"

With no further Plygrange backing 1982 saw Jim back in a Formula One car, albeit in the British championship. He would be driving for Bob Fernley, who became a fan after watching Jim in 1980. "I first met Jim when he was competing in the Aurora F1 series, driving a Chevron F2 car. He won the Oulton Park round in the wet and impressed me enough to sign him to compete for AMCO using the Ensign 180B in 1982."

Jim qualified easily on pole for the poorly supported series and looked all set to win the opening round at Oulton Park, only to be unceremoniously taken out by Arnold Glass's McLaren while lapping the Australian. Glass had been racing since the 1950s and, while quick in his day, had qualified ten seconds

What could have been. **Alan Cox**

slower than Jim at Oulton. On another day the incident would have quickly been forgotten, but it cost Jim the biggest pay day of his career up to that point, an astonishing prize of £50,000.

After that disappointment, Jim and the Ensign proved an irresistible combination. He stormed to victory in the next two events at Brands and Thruxton. In between those meetings Jim shared a Lancia Beta Montecarlo Turbo, run by Vesuvio Racing, with Giuseppe 'Joe' Castellano and Mark Thatcher. The team finished tenth overall and second in class in the Silverstone Six Hours, a round of the World Sportscar Championship.

At Donington Park for round four of the British F1 series, Jim was joined at AMCO by Castellano, an American plastic surgeon. Jim qualified on pole, with an unfamiliar name alongside him. Jorge Koechlin was second quickest in his Williams FW07, and became the first Peruvian to compete in a Formula One race. Jim led the event from start to finish, with Koechlin second and Castellano a commendable third. Jim also claimed fastest lap, at an average speed of just over 106mph. Koechlin had moved to the UK in the early 1970s to pursue his racing career, sharing digs with the late Tom Pryce for a while near Brands Hatch.

With the title already in the bag Jim didn't compete in round five at Brands Hatch. He was there all weekend, however, giving help and advice to Castellano. It clearly worked, as Castellano went on to score an unexpected victory, despite an off in practice. He looked up to Jim himself. "He was a bit of a hero to me. He was so fast and precise. We socialised together with my sons, Vittorio and Dante."

Accompanying Jim that weekend was childhood friend Janet Donnison. "We went to support Joe Castellano. Joe crashed in practice, confirming Jim's belief that I was bad luck for racing drivers! Similar things had happened to Rob Moores and another American friend when I was around. I never went to see Jim race. That weekend he told me he couldn't understand why people went to watch motor racing, for him it was boring. When we went back to the hotel that night, Jim put all the shoes we had by the side of my bed. When I asked him what that was about he said, 'I snore. If I wake you up, throw a shoe at me and you might have time to get back to sleep. Hope you have enough to last the night!'" The final round of the championship didn't even take place. Silverstone officials saw no point in staging a race for so few cars (they usually insisted on

a minimum 15 starters). They preferred to have Formula Three topping the bill and a reduction in ticket prices rather than a tedious finale.

In the years to come, Jim would become a much-valued development driver in America. His ability to diagnose and describe problems was already in demand before his move stateside. Rodney Dodson was one customer who hired Jim for this very reason. "We employed Jim in the early '80s to set up a F2 Ralt for a German driver and tested all day at Donington. He was very quick and brilliant with feedback. We never really negotiated a fee. Jim being Jim just requested us to pay what we thought was fair. I hope he was satisfied with what we gave him." The driver in question was Henning Hagenbauer, and he remembers the occasion well. "Jim did a set-up which suited me well, and was like a team-mate you'd like to have. We had a great day."

At the end of 1982 Jim found time for a working vacation in Trinidad, where he went with Bobby Howlings to race at Wallerfield, which had been a US Air Force base, named after the American World War One pilot, Major Alfred J Waller. Howlings realised there was a market for second-hand racing cars and spares in the Caribbean. There could be no better advertisement for his wares than Jim putting on a demonstration of high-speed driving. "Jim's trip to Trinidad was part of the AMCO motor racing schedule,

Jim strolled to the 1982 British F1 title and is seen enjoying himself here in the Ensign at Oulton Park. **Trevor C Collins**

which my partner Bobby Howlings organised annually," remembers Fernley. "Bobby managed the Caribbean programme, which took place around November each year, and I managed the Indian programme in February."

Bernard Devaney was also on the trip. "I knew of Jim, but the first time I met him was at the airport heading for Trinidad. We just hit it off straight away. The craic started as soon as we got on the plane, and the pair of us got absolutely hammered on the flight across. It was a holiday for us, and the sponsor (British West Indian Airways) was paying for everything. Happy days!" Upon disembarking from the aircraft the duo were in for a surprise. "We went down a tunnel, and around a corner" remembers Devaney. "What greets us? TV cameras and interviewers. There we are, propping each other up!"

Canadian driver Scott Lucas was also competing at the event, having travelled over with a group of racers from Ontario. He remembers Howling's entrance well. "Bob Howlings brought an Opel Commodore to race and sell there. It arrived with a boot full of formula car spares for sale. We nicknamed him 'Smilin' Bob', ever the salesman!" Devaney also remembers Howlings and his wares. "Bob had a lot to do with organising the trip. He was wheeling and dealing, selling cars to the locals. I think he sent over some of the cars that were used. They left a lot to be desired, I can tell you!"

James Weaver turned up, despite not having a drive for the event. Devaney's car, like Jim's, was being provided by a local team. The first time the foreigners set eyes on it was during a visit to a shopping mall, where it was being displayed to help publicity for the meeting. Devaney was not present to see the spectacle, but Lucas was and has never forgotten it:

"The first car we looked at was a March that must have just been moved out of a chicken coup and put on show. It still had feathers and bird guano all over it, with a sign that said 'Do Not Touch.' Jim turned to me and said quietly, 'Do

Jim shared a car with fellow Scot, David Leslie, at a Sports 2000 round in July 1982 at Oulton. This Alan Cox photo was used for a caption competition in Autosport. **Alan Cox**

not touch because you'll get covered in shit.' The sight of this car made Jim a little uncomfortable. It wasn't his, but was this the level of prep to be expected? With great relief Jim's car, further down the mall, was found to be in tip-top shape."

When Devaney did set eyes on his car he was suitably underwhelmed. He was cajoled into going out for practice despite the fact the rear wing was bolted on the wrong way around. When he pulled in and complained of a distinct lack of brakes or suspension the reasons were quickly found. The car had seized dampers and the brake calipers had been fitted upside down. An unimpressed Devaney climbed out and found a use for the rear wing, using it to open a bottle of Coke. When it came time to race he burned out the clutch on the line and walked away. "It was unbelievable," he says. "It was as if it was held together by rubber bands. All the rosejoints were hanging out, what a mess. I was more worried for the spectators, because they were lining the circuit. They were the barriers."

Jim behind the wheel of Vesuvio Racing's Lancia in a successful outing away from single-seaters. **Jeremy Banks**

Waiting on the grid at Wallerfield, a circuit with its own unique challenges. **Gordon Gonsalves**

Celebrating after one of his race wins. This was the only occasion in his career that Jim raced a Brabham. **Boardman Family**

The international meeting was big news locally and the drivers were kept busy with PR work for newspapers, radio and TV. For the races, in excess of 10,000 spectators turned up. Drivers from neighbouring islands also flocked to the track with entries from Guyana, Jamaica, St Kitts and Antigua. "The day after we arrived they had a welcoming party to greet us, including the local Mayor" says Devaney. The TV cameras were there, and we had a good old laugh doing the interviews. We were asked if we'd ever thought about doing anything else. I told the reporter I'd though about becoming a priest – this was printed in a newspaper article! Of course, Jim was standing there pissing himself laughing."

The track itself was smooth, with one noticeable bump before the last corner. The main straight was the old runway and about 12 lanes wide. It had lain unused for some time however, which gave Lucas an unusual problem during practice:

"The underbrush had a chance to grow in. In a tropical climate it grows in fast and thick. It didn't occur to me that I should follow one of the locals around just to find the track. On my first lap, halfway through turn one, the track outline

just disappeared. I found myself driving through the infield, lost! A WTF situation before WTF was known. I made up for it by qualifying second though."

There were races on successive weekends. In between them the visitors were accommodated at a hotel in Port a Prince on Tobago. Devaney couldn't fault their hosts. "The local motor club organised things very well. Its members had us in their homes and at barbecues, that type of thing. We were very well looked after. Between the hotel bills and the drinks I wouldn't like to have seen what it cost the sponsor.

Jim won all the races he was entered for, and Lucas was suitably impressed. "Watching and listening to Jim circulate was a joy. The four downshifts needed for the last corner were just music. Perfect, lap after lap after lap." Local driver Gordon Gonsalves was another left with a lasting impression, after sharing the track with Jim. "I had recently purchased a March 73B, and this would be one of my very early races with a single-seater. It was great racing against someone of Jim's stature and despite, being outclassed by him, it was a feather in my cap to have had the experience."

Chapter Eight

Transatlantic Traveller

Can Am would provide the launching pad for Jim's career in the US. **Author's collection**

Jim globetrotted with Fernley during a busy 1982. In addition to his British F1 commitments, and the trip to Trinidad, the pair also dipped their toes in Can Am waters. Can Am (an abbreviation of Canadian American) was a series for unlimited sports cars, attracting all sorts of weird and wonderful contraptions. By 1982 the championship was in serious decline, a far cry from its heyday in the late 1960s and early 1970s when the works orange McLarens dominated the series. Fernley also managed Jim's career during this period. It was an arrangement which suited Jim well, as Fernley explains. "My management of Jim was only because he was too mean to pay a manager!"

Before crossing the Atlantic, Jim assumed the role of best man for his old team manager Mike Peers. "We were both wearing silvery grey suits and went to the pub before the ceremony," Peers recalls. "To see Jim dressed in a morning suit was just bizarre. The wedding was at St Anne's Square in Manchester and the police had erected barriers there for some event. Of course, when we pulled up in the wedding cars everyone thought someone famous must be getting married!"

Jim was keen to have Mike Peers join him in America, but

his friend eventually decided against the offer. "He rang me and wanted me to go do Can Am. I was working in the family business at the time and had to ask myself where I saw financial security coming from. Motor racing had only ever cost myself and the business money."

Such was the flexibility of the Can Am rules that, providing cars featured covered wheels, almost anything went. With this in mind Fernley decided an ideal car for Jim would be the Ensign Formula One car with specialised bodywork. "We started planning the Can Am programme during the summer of 1982. It was an exploratory six race programme to determine what we wanted to do for the 1983 series."

The transformation of the Ensign from Formula One to Can Am spec took place at the Docking Spitzley team's base. John Connel attached custom designed pontoons to the car, resulting in a striking closed wheel machine. *Autosport* noted that it could be turned back into an F1 car in just 20 minutes.

Jim missed the Can Am race at Riverside. Castellano took over his car for the event after Jim had a stand-off with his team boss. Fernley remembers that, "Jim and I had a difference of opinion on how much he should be paid.

Away from racing, Jim and girlfriend Sue Deakin took the chance to discover the US and North America. Pictured at Disneyland and Niagara Falls. **Sue Deakin**

We never actually fell out about it." Rival John Graham reckons Bob was actually doing his best for Jim by making the switch. "At Riverside Jim was not in the car, but the funds brought by the other driver gave the team the money to put Jim back in the car for the following rounds. I had enormous respect for Bob. I think he would do whatever it took to keep Jim in the car. I always thought he was the big brother Jim needed."

Despite only competing in a handful of events Jim finished the 1982 Can Am season fifth overall in the standings. In the *Autosport* review of the Can Am season he received a glowing write-up from Gordon Kirby. "... Crawford showed his stuff by taking the overweight, under-torqued car to second at Trois Rivières, fifth at Mosport, fourth at Caesars Palace and third at Laguna Seca. In total the team took home some $35,000." The TV commentator at Trois Rivières was impressed by what he saw. "Jim Crawford, in the Ensign Formula One car, crossing the line in second, and I know that his is a name that we'll be hearing much more about."

The compact set-up provided for the team by Ford. **Sue Deakin**

The following year, 1983, would bring a full assault on the title, with sponsorship and assistance from the British carbon fibre specialists RK Fibres. The RK Ensign N180B Jim would use was fitted with a 3.3-litre Ford Cosworth. Jim's biggest rival looked sure to be Jacques Villeneuve (brother of the late Ferrari legend Gilles), driving a well-developed 5.0-litre Frissbee-Chevrolet which had carried Al Unser Jr to the 1982 title. Villeneuve, like Jim, had made his name in Formula Atlantic where he was a double champion.

The first race involved getting the car ready in time to fly out. It finally turned a wheel at Oulton Park on May 26th, albeit sans wings. The very next day it was on a Wardair flight to Canada. The airline offered free transit, with the caveat that the team had to make a scheduled 747 flight on May 27th. Jim felt positive about his chances after the shakedown run when questioned how the car felt. "Well, straight out of the box, so to speak, pretty good. This morning we've probably lapped Oulton faster than anyone has ever been round before – but I think there's still more to come. We'll be able to try a few more tweaks once we're over there."

There had been sizeable investment in the programme, making it imperative Jim was successful and able to win a handsome share of Can Am's lucrative prize fund. The cost of the car and development was put at £100,000. Two engines accounted for £50,000, and the tyre bill amounted to £10,000. The team would, at least, save on transporter costs, with Ford of America supplying a trailer and van. Jim expressed the team's gratitude. "This is a great help to us because of the sheer amount of travelling we'll be doing to get from race to race. All in all, we'll do a thousand miles or so of actual racing and perhaps twelve thousand road miles to get from track to track."

With only six rounds making up the season, consistency and reliability would be crucial. It was June before round one took place, at Mosport. Villeneuve won easily, with Jim

The band of pirates were a happy bunch. Country musician Brian Good on the left, and Jim's loyal mechanic, John Connel, wearing the white hat. **Sue Deakin**

a distant second. The race was marred by a horrific accident which befell Californian driver Mike Lee. He was rushed to Sunnybrook Medical Centre in Toronto, but succumbed to his injuries the following day.

When racing in Canada, Jim stayed with country music star Brian Good, of The Good Brothers. They had got to know each other through another driver on the Can Am trail, John Graham. Good remembers how the link between Canadian musician and Scottish racing driver came about. "I had introduced John Graham to Gordon Lightfoot, on the golf course, and Gordon handed him a cheque afterwards. That was the start of Gordon Lightfoot Racing. John then met Jim at Trois Rivières, and later introduced me to him. We hit it off right away. He liked our music, and came to some of our shows." Graham remembers meeting Jim for the first time. "I met him at Three Rivers, where I was also introduced to Colin Bennett. In 1982, Jim shocked a lot of people with what he did against a strong field. Can Am was weaker in '83, but Jim was the best driver that year, for sure. He upset Villeneuve."

Bob Fernley stayed in a house in Toronto owned by football player Brian Budd which, according to Good, was somewhat notorious. "It was shared by musicians, athletes and racing drivers. It was a party house, with quite a cross section of people." Fernley remembers it well. "The living arrangements in Toronto were great fun. In the house was Brian Budd, who was World Superstars champion, John Graham and a sports radio presenter whose name escapes me. They let me use the spare room when I was in town. As one of my sponsors was the airline, Wardair, I spent a reasonable amount of time in Toronto."

Graham also has fond memories of the house. "Gordon Sweetzer lived there too. He was a football player for Toronto Blizzard, along with Brian Budd. There was also a singer from an Irish showband, who got called 'The Wee Man.' There

were some crazy events at the house, and Jim blended in quite well!"

Jim soon moved out and started living with Good at his coach house a short distance away. Good felt it was a better fit for Jim. "He'd rather be in a quieter atmosphere, but he'd be back at the other house for the parties! Then he would say to me it was time to leave. This was usually because the drink had run out, and he knew I always had a fully stocked bar."

Good was asked by Jim if he wanted to be part of the crew at Mosport, an offer which was readily accepted. "He was second on the grid, sitting in his car under an umbrella, when he got something in his eye. I was putting in eye drops for him when a reporter stuck a microphone under his nose. They asked Jim what his plan was for the race. 'I plan to drive this car, in that direction, as quickly as possible!' During the race I was on the pitboard, the glory job. Afterwards, one of the guys from the Canadian Tire team gave Jim a jacket. He politely accepted it, but when the guy was gone he said, 'I'm not going to wear that bloody thing!' and gave it to me. He also handed me a crash helmet and the huge bottle of champagne from the podium. I still have the helmet, and use it when I'm snowmobiling. I kept the champagne for years. My brothers and I finally opened it to celebrate writing our 200th song."

The Can Am teams reconvened a month later at Lime Rock Park. Jim left the Connecticut circuit with the championship lead, winning the race while Villeneuve was forced out with engine trouble. Rick Crosby was on the crew of a Datsun in the production car class that day (a support event to Can Am), but he was a big fan of Jim:

"I guess the Scottish ancestry in me first made me follow him, just as it did Jim Clark when I was a youngster. I admired his bravery on the track, and campaigning an older, underpowered Ensign Cosworth against Villeneuve's custom-built Frisbee Chevy. My friends also said that, with my longer hair and beard, I resembled him at that time. In fact, that weekend, much to their amusement, I was mistaken for Jim by a young fan at a restaurant!"

Jim's Ensign may have been down on power compared to Villeneuve's mount, but its fuel consumption was significantly less. After his driver's race Crosby managed to remain in the pit area for the Can Am event, positioning himself at Jim's stall where he witnessed the crew do their stuff. "Can Am rules required a refuelling stop and the Cosworth didn't need it. I still remember chatting to a crew member when he excused himself to prepare for a stop, donning a full nomex suit. Crawford came charging down pitlane and stopped. They inserted an empty dump can in the car, instantly removed it, and off he flew. Then they all congratulated each other on the fastest refuelling stop. Priceless!"

> ## Jim was the best driver that year, for sure. He upset Villeneuve

Jim and the Ensign were a constant threat to Villeneuve throughout 1983. **Christopher Mann**

Although down on power compared to their main rival on track, precious time could be made up in the pits. **Christopher Mann**

The next race at Elkhart Lake produced a surprise winner when John Fitzpatrick claimed top honours in a fuel restricted Porsche 956 Group C car. Jim had a miserable day, retiring near the end of the race. The weekend was certainly memorable for David Free, crew chief for Roehrig Racing. "Jim almost ran me over as he was coming up pit road. Someone stepped out in front of him, forcing him to steer hard left and then hard right. I was at the pitwall with our pitboard and the timing guy. I closed my eyes and felt my pant leg move. After the race I spoke to Jim and we laughed about it. He gave me a bottle of his sponsor's whisky. He was a super nice guy."

From there it was on to the spectacular Trois Rivières street circuit in Quebec. It was here that Gilles Villeneuve first came to the attention of Formula One teams when he soundly beat invited Grand Prix drivers in an Atlantic event. In 1983 his younger brother Jacques achieved the same outcome in Can Am, winning by over a lap. Jim somehow dragged the Ensign round to finish second, despite crashing in the pitlane.

Showing there were no hard feelings after their collision on the other side of the Atlantic earlier in the year, Jim took the March 811 driven by his Oulton Park nemesis Arnold Glass out for a few laps to try and sort it. It was to no avail, as Glass failed to qualify. Jim also found himself back in a pure single-seater, practising a Ralt RT4 Atlantic car

Jim turned a few laps in this Formula Atlantic Ralt. **Gladiator Road Racing**

entered by Rick Shea, although he did not take part in the race itself.

Jim's second win of the season came in the penultimate round, back at Mosport. Villeneuve trailed him home, setting up a title decider at Sears Point with Jim leading the standings by a single point. The Sears Point track, in Sonoma, California, was a new one to Jim. On the Wednesday preceding the race he completed 30 laps of it in a borrowed Ford Thunderbird. One of the main issues he found was frequently changing grip levels. "There are five different surfaces," Fernley told journalists. "That presents tremendous handling problems and some of the circuit is breaking up."

The season finale lived up to expectations. Villeneuve looked to be heading for a comfortable victory and the title, but then the rain came. Jim started reeling in his rival, in a drive reminiscent of his famous Aurora win at Oulton Park three years previously. This time it was not to be. The rain eased and Jim found some backmarkers thoroughly uncooperative. The two protagonists finished the race in the same order they occupied in the final standings. Villeneuve was champion, with Jim a despondent second. For Fernley it was a frustrating weekend:

In conversation with Canadian driver, the racing doctor, Charles Monk. **Christopher Mann**

Jim waits on the grid at Oulton Park, ready to delight spectators with the never-to-be-forgotten sound of the rotary B16. **Chris Higginbotham**

Chasing Tiff Needell's Fittipaldi in the British Open F1 series at Oulton. **Alan Cox**

At speed in the ungainly looking March. **Dan Wildhirt**

"Although Jim and Jacques traded fastest laps throughout the qualifying period Jacques' Frissbee was better suited to the Sears Point track. A rain shower allowed Jim to close in the race and at one point he managed to pressure Jacques into a mistake but could not capitalise on the opportunity. Shortly after, the rain stopped and Jim couldn't get on equal terms again." Nevertheless, Fernley reckoned it had been a sterling effort by Jim and the small team around him. "We've proved our point. We've come over on a limited budget and led the series for most of the season."

John Graham saw another side to Jim during their time racing in Can Am, a harder edged version than when away from the track or in non-racing company. "He was friendly and sociable, but he wasn't going to help me as a driver. I think the social setting we were in was very casual, and the racing scene in North America was very friendly. I think this caught Jim off guard to begin with. I don't think he was warm and cuddly with any driver." On one occasion Jim let his frustration get the better of him, regarding Graham's sponsorship and funding courtesy of Gordon Lightfoot, the renowned singer-songwriter. It led to a tirade from Jim against the Canadian driver in a hotel room. Graham put it down to a mixture of alcohol and pure resentment, knowing that, with similar funding, he could be winning regularly.

In between his Can Am commitments Jim returned to Britain to partner his great friend Barrie Williams in a rotary Chevron B16, a car once heard never forgotten. The laid-back duo competed in the domestic Thundersports series, although Jim's only victory came partnering old Atlantic rival David Kennedy in a Ford C100 at Donington Park. He also appeared as a Libre entrant in the only round of the British Open F1 series, which took place at Oulton Park, only to retire with fuel issues after seven laps.

Back in North America Jim's main title rival for the 1984 Can Am championship was Irishman Michael Roe. He would again be driving a VDS for Don Walker's Dallas Motorsports team. It was a proven and well sorted car, but

Roe remained wary of Jim, who would be getting used to a 5.0-litre March 847 which had been designed and built for the team in the UK. "I always think intelligence wins motor races, and Jim has all the intelligence you need to be a very, very good racing driver."

It was during this time that Jim became friendly with Tommy Byrne, a very colourful Northern Irishman blessed with an extraordinary talent for driving racing cars. Byrne would briefly race in Formula One, and tested for McLaren, an event which has passed into racing folklore, as the rookie smashed the best lap times of the team's two race drivers at Silverstone.

"Jim, Michael Roe, myself and the wives all hung out together when we lived in Dallas. There was a lot of partying. When Jim moved to Florida we would go visit him before we eventually went our separate ways, and I didn't see him for a while after that."

The 1984 Can Am season quickly developed into a rather predictable pattern, despite the end of season points table suggesting it had been a close battle. Roe proved untouchable in the VDS and swept to seven wins, out of the ten events. On all seven occasions Jim came home second, and picked up three wins himself when Roe hit trouble.

A particularly fortunate win fell into Jim's lap at Trois Rivières in early September. After qualifying second Jim held on as best he could to the rapid VDS, but was over four seconds down after 30 laps. With just seven laps to go Roe suddenly slowed, having broken a driveshaft on the tough street circuit. Jim swept by, but even then almost didn't claim the win. With only a couple of laps left he tried to put a lap on Horst Kroll, only for the Canadian to turn in on the March and damage its front wing. Jim continued in more circumspect fashion, aerofoil askew, to finally take the chequered flag. The track announcer used his Sunday name at the podium presentation. "From Bolton, England, James Crawford!"

Jim's other two wins that year came at Road Atlanta in

August, and in the closing round at Green Valley Raceway, Texas. By then his mind was firmly on other challenges. Can Am was a mortally wounded animal, and Jim's future lay elsewhere.

Jim's final season in Can Am came in 1984, and it was a period of his life he would later look back on with great affection:

"We put the car on a plane, rented a truck and a trailer, and did five races – Montreal, Toronto, Las Vegas, Riverside and San Francisco. I finished in the top four in all of them, made a whole bunch of prize-money, and thought this was the place to be… It's the excitement of getting in a truck and driving across America. Just getting from race to race was an adventure." While the 1984 Can Am season had proved frustrating, Jim had found the time at the start of the year to enjoy himself racing in India. The plan was for Jim to drive the car, in addition to a Chevron Formula Two machine at the meeting. Their efforts were followed by a Channel 4 film crew for an hour-long documentary.

The Grand Prix in Madras was a remarkable affair, held over two weekends on an airfield circuit at Sholavaram and featuring an eclectic range of machinery. Approximately 300 entries were received, competing in races for bikes, cars and karts. It was organised and run by the Madras Motor Sports Club, which had been founded in 1953. Curiously, the catalyst for the formation of the club came from a race between an Englishman and an Italian. Jim's cars bore sponsorship from McDowell's No 1, a brand of whisky made by United Breweries. Mallya had won the single-seater event in 1982 and 1983. Paul Dunnell made the trip from the UK to India twice. In 1984 he was at the wheel of an Argo Formula Ford 2000:

"The event was arranged by Vicky Chandhok. He had secured backing from the Indian government to get some British drivers over and boost the status of the event. The first time I went to race in 1984 I had to pay £500 and for this the car was shipped over. When I went back a couple of years later I was paid to go."

Several other British drivers had made the trip to India to compete in Formula Ford machinery. Wayne Earnshaw, Martin Stone and Paul Mather were also there. Practice on the track was an interesting affair, with a dog wandering around at the hairpin at one point and a saloon having to take evasive action to miss a spectator who was nonchalantly walking across the circuit. Dunnell remembers it as being, "fantastic, but also very chaotic." On one occasion Dunnell went out socialising with Jim and the other British drivers:

"We all went down to Vicky Chandhok's father's house. We went down to the garage and it was full of old

In the main event Jim was untouchable, leading from start to finish

Rolls-Royces, dating back to the 1920s. I had first met Jim in 1978 when he was racing in Formula Three, a series my company was heavily involved in. There were a lot of very good young drivers around at that time. I think he did the clever thing going over to the States rather than chasing a Formula One drive in Europe."

Fernley was a veteran of the Indian event, having first made the trip in 1982 to look after an ex-Nelson Piquet Ensign Formula One car. The car belonged to Mallya, after he had travelled to Cheshire to buy it from AMCO. Mallya used it to win the race and the duo returned in 1983 (this time with a ground-effect Ensign N180B) to repeat their triumph.

Mallya's father passed away before the 1984 event and he was unable to participate due to family business commitments. This was a major blow as Mallya would have been allowed to keep the trophy if he won the event three times. It was at this point that Jim entered the fray, replacing Mallya.

Jim was favourite for the main 25-lap event in the Chevron. His main rival was Vicky Chandhok in another Formula Two Chevron, entered by MRF Racing. In practice, brake problems saw Jim stop out on track and return to the pits on foot, but in qualifying he claimed pole position. Qualifying had its own unique format, with two cars setting off simultaneously. Jim was paired with Chandhok, but the latter had difficulty getting away which left Jim with the circuit to himself.

Race day on the first weekend began with an event for 50cc mopeds. This was followed by a scooter race and then

Celebrating victory at Mosport. **Christopher Mann**

Despite his best efforts, Jim once again finished the season as runner-up.
Christopher Mann

Jim on the grid. **Madras Motor Sports Club**

Jim on his way to victory in India. **Madras Motor Sports Club**

the saloon cars. The field for the latter consisted mostly of Ambassadors. The Formula India cars were next out. These remarkable machines were mostly home built, resembling open-top sports prototype racers. Modified saloons ran in the same event, including Mallya's Fiat. Fernley drove it to get some much needed test mileage, but it lasted only a couple of laps before being sidelined. Preceding the single-seater event was the motorcycle race, which was won by British rider Neil Tuxworth after a spirited fight with countryman Neil Robinson.

In the main event Jim was untouchable, leading from start to finish and building up a huge lead over Chandhok's Chevron. Back in the pits Jim was interviewed for TV:

Interviewer: "You're 1982 British Formula One Open champion. Coming out to India, how do you find the racing out here?"

Jim: "It was better than I was led to believe. The circuit's not too bad, it's just a little bit bumpy but, all in all, it's very well organised. I'm quite surprised, pleasantly surprised."

Interviewer: "You're driving a Formula Two Chevron. How have you found it's performed in this sort of heat and conditions?"

Jim: "Fine. It's a well proven car, the engine's a well proven engine. It was just a case of bolt it all together and drive it. So no problems there at all."

Chandhok was liberal in his praise for Jim. "It was absolutely thrilling to race with him. I enjoyed it. But let me admit my limitations. I tried my best. And I think I did my best. But Jimmy was too quick for me... Well, if you bring John McEnroe or some such powerful player like him to Madras, could you expect a local amateur player to trouble him? You can't."

The second weekend of the meeting didn't start well for Jim. A mosquito bite led to an infection. He elected not to drive the Fiat but to concentrate on winning in the Chevron. Instead, Fernley donned Jim's helmet and took the wheel of the modified saloon, winning his class. As Fernley stepped victorious from the car a laughing Jim was there to greet him. There was a minor scare for the team at the start of the single-seater event when Jim struggled to pull away on his warm-up lap. He made it in time to slot into pole position and was never headed. With Chandhok a non-starter there was no real competition for the Chevron. At the end of the meeting Mallya expressed his satisfaction. "Absolutely wonderful, extremely proud of our performance. Jim of course, as expected, performed wonderfully. Bob in the modified Fiat did an excellent job."

Jim's victory was somewhat overshadowed by a misunderstanding over the rules, as Fernley remembers. "We wrongly assumed that, by the team winning the trophy three times, Vijay could retain it, only to be informed after clarification of the rules that it had to be the same driver."

Undaunted, Fernley made the long trip to India twice more with Jim. Using a Chevron and then a Lola he won the event three times in total. Jim was entitled to keep the trophy, but gave it to a delighted and highly appreciative Mallya.

Chapter Nine

The Start of a Love Affair

Pit stop en route to fourth place. Jim's tyres have picked up a considerable amount of debris on the way in. **David Allen Hutson**

"For Crawford, having been up and down the F1 ladder, Indycars are the logical progression... His kind of dedicated, considered approach would be well appreciated by those in the ranks of CART's PPG Indy Car World Series."

Jim made his CART debut in the 1984 season opening race around the streets of Long Beach. With continued support from United Breweries, Jim was behind the wheel of a Cosworth-engined Theodore, again run by Fernley. The car had been modified for the event, as Fernley describes:

"The Long Beach car was a hybrid, as the rear end featured a Hewland gearbox instead of a Wysman. Eddie Wachs was one of my backers, as were United Breweries. RK were both sponsors and technical partners. I can remember totally reworking the rear end of the car in the UK and flying it and the team out to Long Beach, arriving only the day before practice. We had never even started the car prior to our day of arrival."

The team initially planned to shakedown the Theodore at Silverstone, prior to Long Beach, with Tiff Needell at the wheel as Jim was busy completing his rookie orientation at Indianapolis. Unfortunately the air starter required to bring the Ford DFX to life did not arrive in time and a substitute starter proved unsuitable.

Around the tricky concrete wall-lined circuit, Jim showed great speed and precision, using his untried car to great effect. The race was won by Mario Andretti in a Newman Haas Lola, followed by the Marches of Geoff Brabham and Tom Sneva. Behind Sneva was Jim's Theodore, an astonishing result for both team and driver. Fernley remembers it well. "It was a remarkable achievement to finish fourth, with an equally remarkable night of celebrations – a programme Jim and I were quite practised at!"

Following this impressive start, Jim made his way to Indianapolis for his first taste of America's greatest race. Donald Davidson is the track historian at the Speedway, celebrated for his encyclopaedic knowledge and ability to recall obscure facts instantly. Having not missed the 500 since first attending in 1964, British-born Davidson has seen countless drivers come and go during the month of May. Despite this, Jim was someone who stood out to him from the very beginning. "I actually met Jim in 1984, when his outward appearance bordered on alarming! He looked pretty ferocious with his full beard and wild hair, so what a surprise to find him to be such a gentle and likeable person." Davidson would come to know Jim well during

Making an immediate impression on his CART debut at Long Beach.
David Allen Hutson

Jim waits to go on track at Indianapolis. **Rob Neuzel**

his career at Indianapolis. "I did several talks with him, one of which entailed a trip by car with just the two of us – I drove! During it, he revealed quite a bit about himself, especially on the way home. We sat down for chats on many an occasion."

Speaking in April, Jim was upbeat and optimistic about his chances of qualifying for the 500 in his rookie year. "The mechanics are pretty hardened old-timers, and I'm an old veteran myself. There is no reason we should get psyched out. Still, when he got there the Speedway was unlike any track Jim had ever raced on before. He realised immediately that the two-and-a-half-mile, rectangular layout, presented a daunting challenge. "I thought the place was a bit strange, the first time I saw it. You walk down to take a look at Turn One, and you think you'll be hard on the brakes and changing down about three gears. Then somebody says no, you do it flat out. You think they must be crazy. But they're right."

Jim sailed through his rookie test at Indianapolis and by May 8th was lapping at just under 195mph, about 12mph shy of the fastest time set by Penske's Rick Mears. By the end of the week Mario Andretti had topped 212mph, while

Jim was struggling to break the 200mph barrier. The US media had been quick to pick up on the fact Jim was from not only the same country, but the same region, as another Scotsman who had endeared himself to America – the great Jim Clark. Several newspapers made the link between the two men, including *The Indianapolis News*. "His initials are the same as the great Jim Clark. He hails from the same area of Scotland. And, like Clark, he drove for Colin Chapman and Lotus."

Pole Day only brought frustration for Jim, as three laps under 200mph resulted in his team waving the qualifying attempt off. He would have to wait until the next day for another go, but this time he didn't even make it on track. Rain showers had delayed running, but Jim's Theodore was well placed at the head of the qualifying line. Unfortunately, scrutineers deemed that the sidepods had failed a deflection test and the car was removed.

The team still held on to hope, but the car clearly wasn't performing properly. Fernley and his team set to work on it. "We changed everything we bloody well could. We changed the fuel tank, the manifold. We tried everything we could to make it work right." It was to no avail, with Jim

Despite failing to qualify the experience gained was useful, and Jim knew he had unfinished business at the speedway. **Rob Neuzel**

In discussion with Michael Andretti, who would end the month as Rookie of the Year. **Rob Neuzel**

In the March at Laguna Seca. **Dan Wildhirt**

only able to run a couple of practice laps during the hottest part of the day on May 19th. The team hoped to try again late on, when cooler temperatures would give Jim the best chance of making the field, but the gun to end the session went off before they got the chance. It would turn out to be their final opportunity, as persistent rain arrived on May 20th – final qualifying day – and the field stayed as it was.

Jim had one more outing in the Theodore, at Meadowlands in New Jersey. He qualified 26th and was classified 21st, despite retiring with broken suspension. Jim's only other CART appearance came at Laguna Seca, this time in a March 82C entered by H&R Racing. He finished the race 23rd and the season overall in 27th place, thanks to 12 points from Long Beach.

For Jim, the 1985 CART season began exactly as the previous one had, with a fourth-place finish at Long Beach, on this occasion driving a Lola for the tiny Wysard team. After taking a refresher course at Indianapolis, Jim set about making the field, after the disappointment of the previous year. This time he appeared to have done all that was required, averaging 205.269mph for

> ## With no back-up car, Jim looked to have missed out on the 500 again, until salvation arrived in an unlikely form

his four-lap qualifying run on Pole Day. "I'm very relieved. This is the most nervous I've been before a race in the 12 years I've been racing. The atmosphere here is incredible. It really does get your attention."

The team's joy was short-lived. During post-qualifying checks the scrutineers found the Lola to be underweight. Jim's time was annulled and the car eliminated. Jim was crestfallen. "The bottom has just fallen out of my world."

With no back-up car, Jim looked to have missed out on the 500 again, until salvation arrived in an unlikely form. Jacques Villeneuve's Canadian Tire team offered to sell an entry space to Wysard, which enabled them to acquire a new Lola (a car originally intended for another team, but they were having financial difficulties). Carl Hungness described it in *The 1985 Indianapolis Yearbook* as "a curious alliance." So it was that the team running Jim's old Can Am rival rescued his Indianapolis 500 dream.

Of course, Jim still had to qualify the new car. By May 16th he was lapping at just under 205mph. On Saturday 18th Jim was satisfied with a qualifying run of 205.525mph in a

Jim during his first Indianapolis 500 in 1985.
Author's collection

Jim flashes along pit lane in 1984, past the cars of fellow non-qualifiers Ed Pimms and Desiré Wilson. **Rob Neuzel**

Jim (34) in good company on the streets of Long Beach. Danny Sullivan (4) alongside, with Michael Andretti (99) and Al Unser (5) chasing. Further back are Josele Garza (55) and Tom Sneva (2). **David Allen Hutson**

car which the team made sure was well over the minimum weight limit. Jim remarked that it "will probably break the scales it's so heavy!"

Jim's time saw him comfortably make the field in 16th position, on the outside of the ninth row. Alongside him were veterans Johnny Parsons and Chip Ganassi. Jim's race got off to a bad start when his pits to car radio failed shortly after the green flag. For the rest of the afternoon he struggled with acute understeer and lost two laps due to a refuelling problem. The Lola eventually gave up for good on lap 142 with an electrical problem. Jim was classified 16th overall, earning $72,368 for his efforts during the month. He was his usual undramatic self in post-race interviews. "I didn't have any major dramas. The car pushed badly from day one. All the minor events thwarted my steady plodto the finish."

Shortly after Indianapolis Jim was reunited with his Can Am car, at the Kansas City Grand Prix. Held in Penn Valley Park it featured a mixture of modern and classic

racing. Between races Jim turned a few crowd-pleasing demonstration laps. He made four more starts for Wysard during 1985, but never came close to repeating the Long Beach result. His best was a ninth-place finish at Meadowlands.

For Indianapolis in 1986, Jim initially looked set to drive a Lola for the Pace Electronic/Raynor Doors team, but the ride ultimately went to Dennis Firestone. The split between the two parties was somewhat acrimonious. "Crawford alleged Firestone bought the ride with sponsorship money; a source close to the team stated Crawford made unreasonable contractual demands of the low-budget outfit."

Whatever the truth, Jim seemed destined to miss out on the great race. That was until events in a Florida court room changed everything. On May 7th, John Paul Jr was sentenced to five years imprisonment by a judge in Fort Lauderdale, having been found guilty of racketeering charges. His plea to have his incarceration delayed until after the 500 fell on unsympathetic ears.

This left a March-Buick without a driver. The car was a works entry run by Roman Kuzma and Keith Leighton's Teamkar International (the 'kar' part being an abbreviation of Keith and Roman). Kuzma was just coming to the end of his role as the North American importer for March. Although of Estonian descent, Kuzma had grown up in England, just a few miles from Silverstone, before the family emigrated to America when he was 15. Leighton had worked with Jim at Lotus over a decade earlier. His father, Aubrey, was the British stock car champion in 1957 and credited with introducing kart racing to the UK. It was Leighton who recommended Jim for the ride, as Kuzma remembers:

"Robin Herd, the owner of March, left it up to us to find a replacement. Keith had worked with Jim and Lotus and the two struck up a good relationship. Both very much cut from the same material, they got along very well. We called Jim and he was on the next plane."

The ASC March (left) awaits its driver in pitlane, with an umbrella placed to keep the Indiana sun from warming its cockpit. Also in shot is the car of Jim's future team-mate Johnny Rutherford (21) and Dick Simon's Duracell entry. **Rob Neuzel**

Painting of Jim at Indianapolis in 1986 by Scottish artist Amy Briggs, showing the helmet decal he carried for his friend. **Author's collection**

Jim was delighted to be given another opportunity to prove himself in the 500. "I got a call late last night in Dallas saying, 'Can you jump on a plane and be here in the morning?' I wasn't really expecting it; this car never even came into mind."

Kuzma remembers that Jim's seat was in demand. "We had two or three people with quite lucrative deals come to us within hours of talking to Jim, but we stuck to our guns. There was no way we were going to let him down. There was no money involved with Jim."

Jim's team-mate for the month was the experienced Hawaiian, Danny Ongais. Late in the day on May 8th, Jim took the ASC (American Sunroof Corporation) March out for the first time, quickly getting up to over 206mph. Tino Belli was the chief aerodynamicist at March and was having his first proper experience of race engineering an open-wheel car. Belli was immediately impressed by Jim's approach. "He was fucking brave. When he got in the car on the Friday in 1986 he was fast right away. Temporary ill-fitting seat, but he got right down to it." Kuzma was impressed by his new driver's professional approach. "Jim understood all the politics and problems, and was very easy to get along with. Just a good bloke, and a real team player. David Hutson was also at The Brickyard to watch his friend. Jim sported a 'David Hutson Photography' decal on his visor. "Jim put that on as a favour, since he did not have a visor sponsor for the first run at Indy in the Buick."

A recurring theme while interviewing people for this book was Jim's inability and/or downright refusal to publicise himself, but this natural modesty also endeared him to people. Mike Peers recalls that "a lady sent him a sticker and a cheque for $1800 for him to wear it at Indy. He'd never met the woman."

Jim continued practising until his progress was rudely interrupted shortly before 6pm when part of the car's nose became detached in Turn One. The March spun through 720 degrees and struck the outer wall at Turn One with its left rear. The damage wasn't major and Jim was unscathed, although he was made to visit the medical centre twice before being cleared to drive again. He later gave an account of the accident. "As I began to turn into the corner, it just went. I felt something wrong, but there was nothing I could do about it. It was on its way."

Pole Day was Saturday 10th May and Jim showed promising speed in morning practice, lapping at over 210mph. This was still some way short of the leading Penskes, with Danny Sullivan and Rick Mears both averaging over 217mph. The decision was made not to make a qualifying attempt, as Jim explained. "I ran 211 this morning… but I'd hate to have to go out under pressure to go as fast as I can go."

It was on Wednesday May 14th that Jim and the team made a major step forward, reeling off three laps in excess of 214mph. Their joy was short-lived, as on the next lap the engine let go. There was further frustration on Saturday 17th when a lap over 213mph was followed by a turbo failure which also wrecked the engine. The ASC team worked feverishly to install a new V6 fitted with a turbocharger borrowed from Ed Pimm's team, and Jim was back out in the late afternoon for a qualifying effort, only to roll to a halt on his second warm-up lap with a broken hose. The only piece of good luck was that the run was not counted as an official qualifying attempt.

Finally, shortly before 5pm Jim made it into the field with an understandably conservative four-lap average of 208.911mph, good enough for 29th on the starting grid. Jim was both relieved and delighted. "I'm going to take the crew to the pub tonight and buy them a drink. They did a heck of a job."

The 1986 Indianapolis 500 proved to be a long and drawn out experience for everyone involved. Despite every effort being made to dry the track on Sunday 25th intermittent showers ensured there would be no racing that day. Monday was a complete washout, and so the race was rescheduled for the following Saturday.

Jim's career seemed to be back on track by the summer of 1986. **Dudley Evans**

The powerful but fragile March that Jim raced throughout 1986. **Rob Neuzel**

Even when the cars were flagged away on the Saturday a further delay ensued. This was caused by an accident which befell Tom Sneva on the final warm-up lap, when his Skoal Bandit sponsored March-Cosworth turned abruptly left at Turn Two, hitting the inside retaining wall. The rest of the field was brought carefully to a halt on the front stretch while Sneva's car was recovered. Once the track was clear Tony George gave the unusual command, "Gentlemen, restart your engines!"

With a car capable of much more than its 29th grid slot suggested Jim quickly set to work when the green flag was thrown, making up six places on the first lap alone. By the end of lap three the ASC March was up to 19th, and Jim continued his charge. While Michael Andretti and Rick Mears fought a furious battle for the race lead Jim dispatched AJ Foyt and defending winner Danny Sullivan to move up to ninth by the one fifth distance mark.

Ninth was as high as Jim got. He began to slip very slowly backwards, with Rich Vogler sneaking past at the same moment Bobby Rahal was lapping the pair of them. Shortly before the 70-lap mark, Johnny Parsons relegated Jim to 12th, and just after that the smoking ASC car appeared on pit road. A head gasket had failed and Jim's day was finished. He was classified 29th overall, the same position he'd started from. It had been an altogether frustrating month, with the Buick showing itself to be quick but fragile.

Kuzma and Leighton have unhappy memories of the engine situation. According to Leighton, "We went into the race knowing that neither car would reach half distance. Apart from the terrible reliability the fuel consumption was horrendous." Kuzma recalled an extraordinary moment earlier in the month:

"Prechter, who owned ASC, was either in the process of buying McLaren Engines or already had. One Saturday a truck showed up from Detroit, with 15 Buick engines. They were all laid out carefully on our garage floor. A short time later Prechter walked in with the president of Buick and showed him the impressive display. When they left the engines were loaded up again and the truck disappeared!"

Despite these shortcomings Jim was happy to have a drive, and spent his time with the team concentrating on the job in hand. Kuzma admired his driver's approach. "We just had a terrible engine situation. Jim understood all the politics and problems, and was very easy to get along with. He was a driver who had just got a break to get his career back on track, and we were an underdog team with very good personnel. I think we got Jim back in the sport. It's one thing I feel really good about."

Jim's call-up at Indianapolis would prove to be a lifeline for his career. He impressed the Buick personnel and the seed was sown for a long relationship between the two.

Jim loved driving anything fast. With that in mind 1986 would be one of the most interesting years of his career, as he was entrusted with Conte Racing's fearsome March-Buick IMSA car. His partner for the endurance series races was American Whitney Ganz, who already had a season's worth of experience with the car. Ganz knew little about Jim when he arrived:

"Conte Racing was really a revolving door experience. There were all sorts of different drivers in and out. Some were good and some just had money. I didn't know what to expect from Jim and I wasn't really that familiar with him. I guess I knew a little bit about him from his Can Am stuff but, at that point, Can Am was in its twilight so I didn't pay that much attention. You don't really know what's what from the outside looking in. Was it a great car with a so-so driver, or a so-so car with a great driver? Hard to know, so I didn't really know what to expect. He was an unknown quantity to me."

It didn't take long for Ganz to realise that his new teammate was the real deal. Jim already had a great reputation at Buick for his skills as a development driver. Ganz was also impressed by this ability, in addition to his outright speed:

"As a driver he certainly made me work hard. He was fast but his greatest strength was his ability to set up the car. If I remember he had been Lotus's test driver and he was especially good at working with the shocks. I just wanted to go fast! His intuitive understanding of the car in that area always amazed me." Mike Peers backs up Ganz's view. "The great ability Jim had was to communicate what his arse was feeling."

Long-distance races in hot, closed cockpit cars are always a test of stamina. At the 1986 Watkins Glen Six Hours the

> ## The great ability Jim had was to communicate what his arse was feeling

A driver change as Jim takes over from Whitney Ganz in the March-Buick. The two men enjoyed a happy partnership at Conte Racing. **Rob Neuzel**

weather was stifling. It would be a difficult day, made even worse by a piece of technology failing before the start, as Ganz recalls:

"Two minutes before the start, our cool suit system failed and we had nothing on board to drink. We both did the entire race with no cool suits and no fluid on board. It was absolutely brutal. Each time we changed drivers I basically stripped down in the pits to just my underwear and T-shirt and stepped into a large bucket full of ice and water. I also put my hands up beyond my wrists in it, trying to lower my body temperature."

The hard-earned podium at Watkins Glen would be the highlight of Jim's IMSA season. In his other four races that year at Sears Point, Road America, Columbus and Daytona

Jim clambers out of the shattered March after his accident in Miami. **Unknown**

his best result was 16th. Although Ganz and Jim were only team-mates for a short time, he regards a compliment Jim paid him as the greatest he ever received during his racing career:

"I'd like to preface this by saying I had tremendous respect for Jim's ability. As you know, he was always one of the fastest guys at Indy. One day Jim says to me, 'You know, I'm better at setting up the car, but I'm not so sure that if they gave each of us a new set of tyres and put a gun to our heads, you wouldn't be faster.' That was the nicest thing anyone ever said to me during the time I was driving and it meant a lot, especially coming from him."

It was a bad start to 1987 for Jim. On the day before his 39th birthday his mother passed away. She did get to see a video tape of his wedding to Sheila, from her hospital bed. The couple were married near his beloved Lake Windermere. Despite the loss of his mother he did, at least, have plenty of racing to take his mind away from things. Jim was back in the Conte IMSA line-up for 1987, this time driving a Buick-powered March 86G. He was entered for the season opening Daytona 24 Hours, sharing the car with his good friend Tommy Byrne. In the end the car was listed as 'Did Not Arrive.' "I had forgotten all about that," said Byrne. "I may be wrong, but I think that it might have been a money problem with the team.

After the non-appearance at Daytona, Jim finally got to drive the 86G in Miami, where his co-driver was Michael Andretti. The circuit was only just ready in time after local prisoners were brought in to help with preparations. Jim's race ended when he drifted slightly off-line on a fast left-hander and smacked the wall hard. His final appearance in IMSA came at Road Atlanta (Jim was entered at Laguna Seca but was a non-starter), which yielded a 23rd place finish. Events during practice for that year's Indianapolis 500 meant that he would never race in IMSA again.

Chapter Ten

Turn One

In addition to his IMSA appearances in 1986 Jim had continued to pound round in a March 86C, testing for Buick. Between August and November he completed around 1,000 laps at Indianapolis. When Spring testing started for the 500 on April 5th 1987, Jim was again a frequent visitor. He drove on more than half of the 25 test days, more than double the amount of the next busiest driver, Rich Vogler. By the time the track opened for race month on May 2nd Jim's 86C was rumoured to have done more than 4000 miles.

Jim would be driving for the American Racing Series team at Indianapolis, in a car paid for by Pat Patrick and previously offered to Jeff Andretti. The American Racing Series was a championship designed to discover emerging US talent. It was established to solve the problem of the poor state of several junior formulae in the states including Formula Atlantic and CanAm. The series used identical March cars which resembled Formula 3000 machines. Ironically, it was the Italian Fabrizio Barbazza who claimed the first ARS title in 1986. Barbazza was initially meant to drive the Pat Patrick 86C which Jim would eventually pilot. Instead, Barbazza moved to Frank Arciero's team for Indianapolis (Arciero ran Barbazza in the ARS) to replace Randy Lanier, who had gone missing following drug smuggling charges.

Jim's first appearance on track during race month came on May 4th, a day when teams were hampered by high winds. The following day Jim got the car up to an average of 210.3 mph. Meanwhile, Mario Andretti was setting new track records above 218 mph.

A major step forward came on Wednesday 6th May, when the ARS team found a much improved set-up. This allowed Jim to record a fastest lap of almost 216mph on a day when several of his rivals were in trouble. Kevin Cogan, Scott Brayton, Derek Daly and Dick Ferguson all had contact with the retaining wall. Jim's lap time left him well satisfied with the team's work:

"'We were lost at 5 o'clock, stuck at 210,' exclaimed the gleeful Scotsman. 'In desperation, at five till six, we gave

it a big 'tweak' in the pit lane and BANG! It just came right instantly – 5 mph quicker!' Crawford's overall best gunshot of 231 mph sounded even more impressive when it was learned he was running one inch shy of allowable turbo boost."

Over the next couple of days Jim's lap speeds hovered in the 210-214mph bracket. Saturday 9th was Pole Day and the ARS team's plans were interrupted even before Jim got on track, when the March's rear wing was found to be a fraction too high and withdrawn from the qualifying line. When he did finally get out Jim struggled to replicate his practice speed, lapping between 205-206 mph before the attempt was waved off by the team.

It was shortly before 4pm when Jim ventured out for his second attempt at the wheel of the number 2T car. On Jim's mind was his rev counter, which had just broken, making it difficult to judge his speed going into corners. He only made it as far as Turn One on his first flying lap.

"Earlier, I had managed Turn One flat out at 231mph. According to the radar speed measurement I reached 236mph before impact, and in those conditions you cannot judge a 5mph difference." The accident report gives the bare facts of what happened next:

Time: 3:56
Driver: Jim Crawford
Car name: American Racing Series March
Car condition: Extensive damage to right side and front.
Description: Came through the middle of turn 1, spun once 360 feet and hit the wall with the right side, then slid through the south short chute 860 feet. Crawford sustained dislocation and fractures of both ankles and a fracture of the lower right shin bone.

The Indianapolis track is a brutally unforgiving place. Nowadays the oval is lined with the revolutionary SAFER barrier which cushions cars on impact, greatly reducing the risk of serious injury. Back in 1987, the only object to hit was a concrete wall. This meant that foot and leg injuries were

The car is prepared in pitlane ahead of a qualifying attempt which would end in disaster. **Boardman Family**

Nobody had turned more miles at the speedway than Jim ahead of the 1987 event. **Derek Patai**

The March moments after its sickening impact with the wall. The front end damage is clear to see. **Indianapolis Motor Speedway**

not uncommon, but few drivers experienced damage quite as devastating as the Turn One wall inflicted on Jim. Mark Scott's memories of that day are still vivid:

"It's a hollow feeling making that walk to the infield care centre and then on to Methodist Hospital – the 'Crash House' as he and the guys called it – and waiting to see if he was going to be OK. Then, as he's wheeled past us on a stretcher from intensive care to the operating room, he looks up and says, 'I could do with a case of Miller Lite.' His way of assuring us that he'd be OK."

Jim was far from OK, and for a while he stood a very real chance of requiring an amputation. David Hutson rushed to Methodist Hospital, where he remembers breaking down in tears because of the "tremendous and unrelenting pain" being endured by his friend. Hutson was only too aware of the dangers of The Brickyard. In 1982 his close friend Gordon Smiley had perished in a horrifying crash during a qualifying attempt. Jim himself had remained conscious throughout the accident, as he later related. "It took them 10 minutes to burn me out. I remember every detail… the best way to describe it is that the entire front end of the car caved in and my feet came up to my knees." Ron Hemelgarn recalls that "Jim wasn't afraid to stand on the gas. He was really haulin' into Turn One. It was unbelievable."

The immediate outlook was gloomy. Jim's feet and ankles were badly shattered and there was the very real likelihood that he may never walk again. Luckily for Jim he was in the care of Dr Terry Trammell, a senior member of CART's outstanding safety team, along with Dr Stephen Olvey.

Trammell was well used to dealing with serious leg injuries caused by racing accidents. Among the other CART drivers who had benefited from his expertise was Irishman Derek Daly. In 1984, Daly crashed violently during the Michigan 200, the force of the impact ripping off the front of the car and exposing his legs. Daly also knew Jim and gave his observations about his recovery:

"I had my similar accident in 1984 (although Jim's injuries were worse than mine because he had serious orthopaedic injuries to both feet). We were in the same hospital and looked after by the same doctors. This is when we lived three doors down from Jim and Sheila. My impression was that it affected him mentally more than physically. He could not wrap his arms around the injuries."

Tino Belli also has painful memories of that day. "I was working with Michael Andretti. It was a huge crash into Turn One, and I visited him at the hospital that evening. I am not very good with hospitals. Michael also turned up while I was there and all I remember him asking was who pays the medical bills."

Jim later recalled the visit from Andretti, and from Rick Mears. "Rick told me to hang in there. He gave me a bit of support. Michael Andretti also came to see me. It's great to see there are feelings in this sport."

Jim's home for the foreseeable future would be the seventh floor of Methodist. He underwent surgery on the same day as the crash. It would be the first of several surgeries over the following days. As soon as he could, Jim commandeered a wheelchair to get around, visiting other

> He was really haulin' into Turn One. It was unbelievable

Jim looking relaxed during practice in 1987, but after his accident life would never be the same again. **Stephen Sellers**

drivers nearby including Johnny Parsons (who had also crashed at Turn One) and Dennis Firestone, although he did admit, "I'm not really sure what I'm saying with all this medication."

Ironically, Jim's earlier visitors – Andretti and Mears – would both end up in Methodist themselves after crashes that month. Jim was far more familiar with some of his rivals by the end of May. "I didn't know some of these guys too well, but the camaraderie has been great."

Jim was temporarily allowed off hospital grounds on race day, along with Parsons. The two wounded warriors were given VIP treatment, being whisked off to the Speedway to watch the race from an executive suite. For Jim the frustration of missing out on the 500 outweighed his physical injuries. "If I could nail on some new feet I'd be right back out there... You feel bitter that it happened to you for a while, then you feel sad that you're going to miss the race."

Roman Kuzma – his crew chief from the previous year – also visited Jim. "What I remember most was the extent

of his injuries. He was a mess, it was pretty sad. He had a button to push that administered morphine, and he was just constantly pushing it. It would only give out a certain amount per hour but he just kept pushing it, hoping to get some."

When Jim eventually left hospital he was confined to a wheelchair, but he was far from being a compliant patient. A long and excruciating road lay ahead. Metal pins and screws had been inserted into his feet, but straightening his right one would prove to be a major obstacle, not helped by Jim suffering a fall shortly after getting home.

His mood was not helped by problems with the painkilling medication he was prescribed. Still, his many friends did their best to keep his spirits up. Mark Scott was a regular visitor to the Crawfords' house at Morse Lake, Indianapolis. Scott recalls helping to make a wheelchair ramp for his friend on one occasion. Jim was particularly frustrated that he could no longer drive his favourite road car, a replica of the fearsome Porsche 935. Kuzma remembers that Jim had another complication from the crash, namely brake fluid which had entered his bones.

The next few months saw Jim make regular visits to a hyperbaric chamber, in a bid to speed up the healing process. In total he would spend around 200 hours in the contraption. Reflecting on the crash, Jim realised he had simply entered Turn One too quickly. "There was no way in hell it was going to go round the corner. I was the last to know."

Despite surgeries over the months and years that followed Jim would feel the legacy of his crash for the rest of his life. Even by the time of the 1989 race he was still severely hampered. "After two years of physical therapy it isn't getting any better, and I presume that it isn't [going to]. In the morning I go to physical therapy and they crank it straight and tape it up like a football player's foot. But I can't stop it from bending under during the day."

During long recuperation, Jim and Sheila found a new home in St Petersburg, Florida. It was next to the water that Jim loved so much. He would remain in the area for the rest of his life, buying a motorboat called *Desafinado* (Portuguese for 'out of tune'). Old friend Ron Hemelgarn, who ran a chain of successful health clubs in addition to entering cars at the Speedway, stepped in to help Jim. "My driver, Johnny Parsons, shattered his feet at the same time as Jim. What I did for both of them was put exercise equipment in their homes. These were upper body ergometers. The idea was to improve circulation, and fuel the rebuilding of the bones. Johnny was quite religious in his use of it, and healed faster than Jim, who wasn't so dedicated to it."

Jim would also regularly invite friends from the UK. Paddy Atkinson remembers being introduced to a pilot friend who flew in the United States Air Force. "He said, 'I'll do a flyaround tomorrow for sure.' He kept his word and, when he got to Jim's house, performed a vertical climb!"

Chapter Eleven

A Lesson in Courage

Mark Scott recalls it as being "probably November" when Jim first sat in an Indycar again. "We spent some time with him getting him comfortable in the car, and the then team owner Kenny Bernstein was very supportive." Bernstein recognised Jim's mental and physical resilience, in addition to what he had contributed to the Buick programme. "After his injuries, we felt if he wanted to do it we owed him that opportunity. He had tested the Buick and worked his butt off to make it successful."

Indeed, the team and its sponsors never lost faith in Jim throughout his lengthy recuperation, something he highlighted in an interview with the *Bolton Evening News*. "In March, they were testing at the Speedway and they let me drive a few laps. I learned I could still cope, that my nerve hadn't gone, and that started it all again." Jim's final surgery before the 500 took place in February, and a few weeks later he completed four days of testing at the Speedway, clocking 211mph laps.

Against all odds Jim's name was on the entry list for the 1988 Indianapolis 500. Although it was widely known Jim would be driving, the official confirmation didn't come until a press conference was called on May 7th. Few people expected him to finish the race given that he still couldn't walk unaided and the assumed fragility of the Buick V6 he would be using. The chances of a decent result in a year-old car appeared slim. Jim would be at the wheel of a Lola T87/00 dating from 1987, entered by American drag racing legend Kenny Bernstein under the King Racing banner. Bernstein was in no doubt about what convinced him to put his faith in Jim, despite the legacy of his injuries from the previous year. "The biggest quality that attracted me to Jim was

"Few expected him to finish the race"

He may not have been able to walk unaided, but Jim's speed in the car was undiminished. Stephen Sellers

the fact that he was fearless, absolutely fearless." Jim's answer to one journalist's question demonstrated that his sense of humour had certainly not been affected by the crash. When asked if he would have had a chance of pole position in 1987 he replied, "Yes, if I would have done the other ten corners."

David Gill – a friend from Bolton – visited Jim around this time and was incredulous when informed of his intentions to compete in the 500. "I said to him, 'You can't fucking walk!' His reply was, 'That's not really the point of a motor race.'"

Jim relied heavily on his cane to get around the pit area. He also had at his disposal a golf cart. This was at the centre of a story related by Alex F Yovanovich in *The 1988 Indianapolis 500 Yearbook* which showed just how shy Jim could be when it came to confronting strangers. "Jim is a very humble man and this is the demeanour he always carries around. One day, during practice, Jim walked the entire length of pit road on his cane, because he was too embarrassed to ask two women who were sitting on his golf cart to move."

Jim qualified his Lola at 210.564mph, but it was far from a trouble-free run. "The wind was treacherous in the back, and I almost lost it once or twice in Turn Four. That turn was the closest call I've ever had at Indy. Thank God I quit smoking, because now I can hold my breath for all four laps."

In his younger years – including his time in F1 – Jim had been a dedicated smoker. Driving for a team sponsored by John Player Special cigarettes ensured he was kept well stocked. Janet Donnison recalls Jim's parsimonious ways leading to him eventually quitting. "I remember the night he gave up smoking. We were at Dave Gill's after a day out, and we ran out of

During practice in 1988, with the team still to pick up some additional sponsors. **Author's collection**

cigarettes. Jim and Mike Peers made a bet. The first one to smoke had to pay the other one £50. I don't think either of them smoked again!"

Back at Indianapolis, Jim's four-lap average was good enough for 18th place on the grid. Up front, Roger Penske's team dominated proceedings and had all three cars on the front row. On race day it remained to be seen whether Jim's legs would be up to the task of lapping the famous old circuit

On his way to a remarkable sixth place, which could have been even better. **Author's collection**

200 times. For pit stops he would have to use his left foot on the brake pedal, as his right one was too weak.

Bernstein had flown in from a drag meeting in Memphis and was elated for his driver. "It's a wonderful thing to see Jim come through something like this after watching his dedication through rehabilitation of his legs." Jim reflected on his road back to the 500:

"The first thing I thought when I regained consciousness was, 'I can't let this place beat me like that.' When I found that I could walk again after my [skin graft] surgery in February, I knew I would be back. After all, I had to come back. Otherwise, I couldn't have found a proper job."

After a trouble-free start, the Mac Tools-sponsored Lola began to move steadily through the field until Jim found himself in second place. The early stages of the race were dominated by Penske's Danny Sullivan. Shortly before half distance the caution flag was thrown while course workers set about retrieving a stray drinks can that was rolling around the track surface. Sullivan took the opportunity to dive into the pits for fuel, handing the lead of the race to Jim. He became the first Scotsman to lead the Indianapolis 500 since his namesake Jim Clark in 1967. When racing got underway again, Jim kept the lead until he too was forced to pit. He spent eight laps in the lead, during which time the American commentators were quick to realise significance of his achievement, in particular Indianapolis legend Bobby Unser:

"Crawford's story – you alluded to his injury – is an extraordinary one. He turned up with a big hole really, the size of a silver dollar, in his right foot, as the result of a qualifying crash here last year... He suffered in immense pain – six, seven months – all through the winter... He was taken to the hospital every day for two hours of therapy. The ride in was so painful he'd sit in the back seat with his legs draped over the front seat, with his wife trying to encourage him. And you can imagine with all that behind him now what he must be feeling leading the Indianapolis 500. Of all the people here, maybe it means more to Jim Crawford than almost anyone."

There is little doubt it was a very special moment both for Jim and Sheila, who watched from the Hulman family suite at Turn Four. The birth of the couple's first child was imminent, and Sheila's obstetrician sat with her throughout the race. Any time a driver is on track is always tense for their partners, and Sheila was no different. "What is it they say? Worrying is like sawing sawdust, right?"

As the laps counted down, Jim continued at unabated speed, confounding those who doubted his stamina and the reliability of the Buick engines. Then, with six laps to go, Jim felt the left-front tyre start to go away. He faced one of the biggest dilemmas of his career. "It was a hard decision to come in. I had two scary moments and I thought I'd try to get around for six laps. But I knew I'd look so stupid if I smacked it into the wall. That's when I knew all was lost. It was a wise decision to come in."

> ### Jim was congratulated by members of rival teams up and down the pitlane

Jim's heartache was compounded when the left-front jammed during his pitstop, resulted in the loss of more than 90 seconds. Rick Mears took the chequered flag in his Pennzoil sponsored Penske for his third Indianapolis 500 victory. The race finished under caution and, directly behind Mears on the track, was Jim. As the cars crawled along pit lane the unofficial classification showed Jim as finishing in second place. Later, when the scorers studied their lap charts, he would be pushed down to fifth. Emerson Fittipaldi then had a penalty rescinded, and Jim was finally classified sixth. When Brian Hammonds interviewed Jim moments after he climbed from his car, however, he was still thought to be second:

Brian: "You just can't say enough about the drive of this man, Jim Crawford. This man's feet are literally... [loud cheers follow the mention of Jim's name, momentarily forcing Hammonds to stop] This man's feet are literally held together by pins and screws, after a terrible accident here last May. This is his first race back, second place. Congratulations."

Jim: "Thanks very much. I'm happy for the Buick people. Well, A, we've done all those miles of testing and, B, they've stuck with me while I was injured. So I feel very happy for them. They deserve it."

Brian: "What about your feet? Did you feel any pain out there?"

Jim: "Eh, they probably hurt like hell, but I won't notice it for an hour or so now."

Brian: "Were you ever competitive with Rick Mears? Do you think you could have caught him?"

Jim: "No, he came past me early on in the race and there

The calm before the storm. Jim's year old Lola awaits its driver. No one could have anticipated what was to follow.
Author's collection

Jim roars away from his pit stall and back into action. He spent far longer than anticipated on pit lane that day, making his achievement all the more remarkable.
Jay Alley

was nothing I could do. I was using all the road and a bit... [laughs] That was as fast as I could go. So, my hat's off to him. He did a great job."

Brian: "One bad thing about it. Your car owner Kenny Bernstein can't be here to enjoy it. He's racing himself down in Baton Rouge."

Jim: "Yeah, I hope he does better than me."

Brian: "That's gonna be awfully hard to do. Jim Crawford, a second-place finish at today's Indianapolis 500."

Rick Mears may have been busy celebrating his victory but, having visited Jim in hospital the previous year, he was full of praise for his rival. "What he's done today is probably good therapy... I take my hat off to him. He did a tremendous job."

Bernstein may not have been at the race in person, but he can still vividly recall the events of that last Sunday in May. "It was just a wonderful day and feeling for the team, and especially for Jim and what he had come through to get back in a race car. He came to the car on pit road in a golf cart and he had a cane to help him get around."

Mark Scott was also under the impression that his driver had finished second, and recalls Jim taking his eventual demotion to sixth with typically good humour. "It was a stuck wheel nut that robbed him of that race, and as the post-race checks went on and we went from second to sixth he said, 'Bloody hell, at this rate I won't have qualified by tomorrow!'" In his race report Donald Davidson summed up Jim's attitude to being bumped down the finishing order:

"A tremendous ovation was afforded the plucky Jim Crawford, who was to occupy four different positions during the next few hours... Was he irritated at dropping a spot every time he turned around? Actually, the extremely pleasant driver was so happy to have finished at all that he just grinned through the whole thing and didn't seem to mind, sympathizing with the complexities of trying to score a race filled with so much confusion."

After the race Jim was congratulated by members of rival teams up and down pit lane. He was particularly pleased when acting legend and team owner Paul Newman tapped him on the helmet and offered him his congratulations

(Newman himself was a very competent part-time racing driver who raced in the Le Mans 24 Hours on several occasions with distinction). Jim's friend David Hutson was also present that day, and witnessed the scenes when Jim finished his slowing down lap:

"When he pulled into the pitlane the crowd erupted in cheers. He was that popular and didn't even try to be. He was quiet, reserved – like most of you Scots – before he got to know you, and was genuinely surprised and happy to wave his cane to the crowd."

The crowd behind Jim's pit had been rooting all afternoon for the quiet Scotsman, which came as no surprise to renowned American motor racing writer Gordon Kirby. "He was the kind of guy people could get behind because he was so genuine."

Kirby was full of praise for Jim in the report of the race he wrote for *Autosport*, and noted a further problem which hampered his afternoon. "Sixth place was the result, then, hardly fitting for the great effort Crawford made at Indianapolis this year. He proved conclusively that he can do the job, even to the point of having to ignore a problem late in the race with one of the screws in his repaired legs coming loose and catching at his suit."

Many miles away, in Alberta, Canada, Jim's friends from the Can Am days, The Good Brothers, were on tour. Brian Good remembers their reaction. "My brother and I were watching the race in the hotel. We were celebrating and dancing around the parking lot!"

In the immediate aftermath of the race Jim was ushered into an empty garage to field questions from reporters on his second-place finish, although everyone present – including Jim – suspected it was an error. "There are very few races where you can spend 90 seconds in the pits with ten laps to go and still finish second. But when the result shows you were second, you don't run up there and say, 'No, I wasn't.' I went to fifth, first, and then about 30 minutes later, I went to sixth. That's when I left the track, just in case."

It had been a monumental effort by Jim and, arguably,

The painting inspired by Jim's comeback drive. **Hector Luis Bergandi**

there was no more popular person that day at the Speedway. For much of the 500 miles he had run the old Lola well below the white line in the corners, extracting every last ounce of performance. Scott remembers that running below the line was something of a Crawford trademark. "Jim actually considered that to be his own. In fact, he was quite miffed when that lower line was grassed over. 'The bastards have grassed over my bit of track!'"

In 1993 Jim spoke to Richard Williams of *The Independent* about his late race pit stop and how much it cost him. "A quarter of a million dollars... Ruined my whole day." It was still, by far, Jim's biggest payday of his Indy career. "I suppose I earn as much as Mrs Thatcher." Jim had further reason to celebrate just a month after his heroic drive, Sheila gave birth to their first child, who they named Jeffrey. He was born in Indianapolis.

On the day following his epic drive Jim decided to treat himself, but nothing too extravagant. Mark Lodge was working in an Indianapolis furniture store at the time. "He came into the store by himself and wanted to try out rocking chairs. I helped him find one he liked and sold it to him. I'll never forget that day. He was as nice as could be. I knew who he was before he came into the store. After meeting him I was even more of a fan."

A postscript to that extraordinary day in May. Jim's 1988 Indianapolis performance inspired engine manufacturer Buick to commission a painting entitled 'A Lesson in Courage.' The painting depicted Jim in the number 15 Lola during a pitstop, and was made into a run of limited edition prints. Mark Scott was unaware of this offshoot from Jim's heroic drive and had no doubt as to what Jim would have made of it. "I don't remember that, but if that's true he would be embarrassed." Hector Luis Bergandi was the artist commissioned by Buick to paint 'A Lesson in Courage'. "I met Jim Crawford at the Speedway, but very briefly. My perception was of having been in front of a rarity, a very brave young man without one cocky bone in his body. His reputation was impeccable."

Chapter Twelve

Getting His Wings and Other Adventures

Following the 1988 race the speedway was completely resurfaced, and Jim was the first driver to try it out at racing speed during tyre testing late that year. He lapped at 212mph and, by the time pre-race testing had finished in April 1989 he was up to 215. The team took their usual thorough and methodical approach, with Jim also putting miles on his back-up car.

With the Month of May underway, it was the second day of practice before Jim appeared, opening day having witnessed a snowstorm. He was quickly up to record stock-block speeds, over 219mph. His performance the following day was even more impressive, as he averaged over 221mph in both his race and back-up cars. Meanwhile, Rick Mears became the first driver over 225 mph in Indianapolis 500 history.

*1989 saw Jim and the team the focus of much press attention. He was always able to put on a smile for the camera, despite any troubles. **Author's collection***

got them watching you, then you must be doing something right."

With the car safely qualified all that was left to do was log some more practice laps before race day. Jim was doing just that on Thursday, May 18th, when a suspension failure sent him into the Turn Three wall very hard. The car lost three wheels in the crash, suffering severe damage to a bulkhead and on the right-hand side of the tub. Jim was briefly unconscious but got away with just a sore hand. The 1985 winner, Danny Sullivan, was amazed. "I can't believe he walked out of that crash. It hurt me just watching."

Jim made the mandatory trip to the care centre for a check-up after the shunt but seemed unperturbed by his ordeal. One journalist shouted a remark to him as he left the centre about it being

Jim's impressive progress continued, although one day was lost completely to the wet weather. On May 11th he battled strong winds to end the day fastest of all. He described how his car was "300 to 400 revs different from one straightaway to the other." On May 12th Jim stunned everyone by turning a lap of 225.960mph. The laptime in itself was controversial as several timing systems recorded it as 226.280mph. "It's working quite well now" was Jim's summation.

Qualifying itself began a day late due to rain washing out Pole Day. Jim's legs were still feeling the effects of the '87 crash. "When it's cold and rainy they stiffen up a little bit." Practice proved troublesome for Bernstein's team as Jim's Lola suffered engine problems. A change of engine was effected, and it was mid-afternoon before Jim got his chance to qualify. He later admitted to making a mistake with his boost setting but still averaged over 221mph for the four-lap run, good enough for fourth on the grid behind pole-sitter Rick Mears, Al Unser Jr in another Penske and Emerson Fittipaldi's Patrick Racing example. All things considered, Jim was quite happy with his lot. "It's a great honour to be up there with the Penske cars... when you've

a good thing he didn't hit the wall feet first. Jim's reply was typically humorous. "Yeah, head-first, much better!" Susan Arnold was working in public relations for the team. "Upon his return to the pits he said, 'I feel like a James Bond cocktail, shaken but not stirred.' I remember that all these years later."

The car itself was in much worse shape, which was a major problem for Jim and the team. They could use the back-up machine for the race, but it would mean forfeiting their hard-earned fourth place on the starting grid. The decision was made to ship the badly damaged tub back to Lola in the UK and hope the crew there could perform a miracle.

As soon as the tub was delivered to the Lola factory, feverish work began on it. Mark Scott recalls that, "Jim was well liked at Lola, and that car had been very quick against newer machinery. The boys in the Lola factory were keen to see it take its rightful spot on the grid."

On May 24th – less than a week after the accident – the tub was back in the US. Bernstein dispatched his crew to collect it from Chicago's O' Hare airport, equipped with a radar detector to prevent any hold ups from speed cops.

Jim was flying in 1989, until bad luck intervened after a tremendous qualifying run. **Author's collection**

For the second year running Jim was involved in a remarkable comeback, but this time it was the car, not the driver, at the centre of it. Note the unpainted black bodywork as the rebuilt Lola takes to the track. **Author's collection**

Bob Abdellah dealt with public relations for the team and described the mercy mission. "When the guys who went there to pick it up explained what it was for, they gave the guys in customs a few racing hats and suddenly it was ready to go.

"The prodigal Lola arrived in Indianapolis at 8:58 Wednesday night. Jim Crawford's qualified Lola tub was hustled to the King Motorsports garage and the well-rested crew began an all-night re-assembly process using parts and pieces from the backup Mac Tools Lola. Crawford had attached a note onto the tub beseeching the Lola personnel to 'Please fix my race car.' The tub returned with a reply reading, 'We did and good luck,' plus a masking-tape banner that said, 'Miracles take a few days. The impossible a little longer.'"

For the second year in succession Jim was the centre of attention at the Speedway as fans followed his battle against the odds. For Kenny Bernstein, the cost of repairing Jim's car would be more than the asking price for a brand new 1989 Lola chassis. Joseph Siano described the scene in the Bernstein garage in an article for *The New York Times*:

'A table in the corner of the garage was laden with fresh fruit, cookies, brownies and pastries to keep the crew well fed as they worked. During the long hours, local television crews stopped by to do live reports for the late evening news broadcasts.'

To the amazement of Gasoline Alley Jim was able to take to the track for Carburation Day, the last opportunity to practice before the race. Bernstein estimated that the combined efforts of his crew and the Lola factory in England had amounted to between 300 and 350 man hours. Showing no sign of fear, Jim soon had the rebuilt Lola lapping at a shade under 215mph, much to the crowd's delight. Although Jim's new mount used the original tub most of the car was

Phoenix saw Jim make a rare appearance away from the Brickyard. **Unknown**

put together from parts cannibalised from the backup machine. Jim noted the irony in this. "It's interesting because 90 percent of the car I ran today was parts from our (back-up) car. It's just a matter of doing things by the letter of the law."

Jim's statement is backed up by Lola designer Bruce Ashmore, who received the chassis in England and supervised the repairs:

"The tub was technically a write-off. We would never send anything back into service that wasn't 100 percent both from a safety and performance point of view. We actually took the whole tub apart and put a new top on it, new side panels and new floor. I remember we used the same seat back panel, dash panel and inner panels but the other bulkheads were new. We were careful to keep the same chassis plate and USAC Tech stickers. USAC had so much power in those days, so we worried about making the chassis look too new. It was actually a new tub by the time we'd finished with it."

Close examination of the wrecked Lola had identified metal fatigue as the most likely cause of the suspension failure. With that in mind the rebuilt car was reinforced in potentially vulnerable areas. Despite much of the car's components having changed and it being assembled with great urgency, Jim had no qualms about the work of his crew and the integrity of his 'new' ride. "Remember when DC-10s kept falling out of the sky? Now it's the safest plane in the air. I think my race car will be the same."

Jim may have been happy with his car, but when questioned by a reporter about his prognosis following the insertion of three steel rods into his right leg after the previous year's crash, he seemed uncharacteristically irritable, having read a newspaper article on the subject. "According to today's paper, there's no way to get them out. He's put them in there and now there's no way to get them out. It's a hell of a way to find out, isn't it?"

On race day, Ashmore visited Jim's garage in the morning and was surprised by just how relaxed his driver was. "He was telling stories about the crash and previous crashes. He was in a light-hearted mood and was also telling us about his boat business. I remember thinking what a great attitude to life this guy has. He was making everyone laugh in the garage that morning."

Jim started the race from the inside of row two, with Mario Andretti and Scott Brayton alongside. After losing a few places at the start Jim ran comfortably in the top ten for the first 130 laps, moving up to fourth. Fans eagerly followed his progress, only to be dismayed on lap 136 when the Lola limped into pitlane with terminal clutch failure. Jim had been struggling for much of the race with the problem, the Bernstein crew having to push start him at pit stops. If the car had held together a top three finish looked a distinct possibility. Once again the speedway gods had deserted Jim.

With Bernstein missing the 1990 Indianapolis 500, Jim

A sequence of photos capturing Jim's dramatic airborne crash. **Author's collection**

found a berth at John Menard's team, where he would have two 1989 Buick powered Lolas at his disposal. The year didn't get off to the best start when Jim crashed during February testing at Phoenix International Raceway, fortunately without injury. In April – also at Phoenix – he started his first race outside of Indianapolis since 1987, qualifying 20th only to suffer an electrical problem in the race which curtailed his afternoon.

At Indianapolis in March Jim had managed 217mph in testing, with the team confident of challenging for the front row in qualifying come May. Jim's team-mate was initially meant to be Steve Barclay, but the Californian's hopes were extinguished by a crash during his Rookie Orientation Programme on April 27th. A suspension failure in Turn

> Jim had the dubious distinction of being the first driver to smack the concrete wall

Two resulted in a very serious accident, with Eddie Cheever stopping his car and running to the unconscious Barclay's aid. Barclay suffered numerous injuries, but thankfully none proved life-threatening. George Snider was briefly in the seat, only to have a change of heart. Finally, Gary Bettenhausen was signed. Things got even more complicated when Rocky Moran's Gohr Racing team agreed a deal with John Menard for Buick engines and other support.

The early running at the Speedway was somewhat overshadowed by a row growing in the background over new rules which mandated older cars (pre-1990) had to run with a diffuser. Teams were discovering that – in addition to struggling to match the times of the new machines – the pre-'90 cars were displaying an alarming habit of getting

At speed in 1990. The replacement nosecone tells us this was taken after Jim's spin before qualifying. **Author's collection**

away from drivers, resulting in several heavy crashes.

Jim had the dubious distinction of being the first driver to smack the concrete wall on May 6th when he crashed in Turn One while still warming up. "I was just working up to speed when she just bottomed out, the wheels left the ground and away she went!" He was uninjured, although the Lola suffered suspension damage and he would be in the back-up car when he returned to action. Prior to his crash, Jim had recorded a 215.6mph lap and had been clocked at over 227mph through the speed trap.

After several accidents involving pre-'90 cars a meeting was called on the evening of May 9th, with many car owners and drivers present. Among those to be caught out by the new specification was Indianapolis veteran Johnny Rutherford, twice. The second shunt landed him in hospital. Spokesman Vince Granatelli made the anti-diffuser brigade's feelings clear. "We've had seven [actually six] accidents in the last three days, all in '89 and older cars. We've had several testing accidents in the past and we just think something should be done. The most important point is that these [older] cars are not as safe now as they were with the exit diffusers out."

May 10th was not a day for high speeds, with cool temperatures and winds gusting over 30mph at times. While others sheltered, Jim was one of the few to venture out in the blustery and dangerous conditions, still in his number 15T spare car. He ended the day with a fastest lap of 208.686mph. To put it in context, Tero Palmroth was next quickest at 203.362mph and the only other driver to manage a lap over 200. Jim had pulled on all his experience of lapping the circuit in difficult conditions during testing. "I had to use caution in turns two and three, but I could blast up and down the front and back stretches. We've tested here in worse conditions, but it's usually snowing as well as blowing on days like this!" On the same day USAC and IMS also delivered their verdict on the diffuser controversy. There would be no change to the regulations.

The following day saw Jim back in the news for the wrong reasons, as he took his rebuilt primary car out. Once again, the malevolent Lola bottomed out in Turn One. What unfolded produced some of the most iconic images ever captured at the Speedway. Jim's car slammed into the wall before launching itself over one of its flailing tyres and taking flight. After reaching an impressive altitude of

> # Jim attended a ceremony where he was presented with his Wings of Gold by the US Navy

around 15 feet Jim was returned to earth with the car the right way up. Despite his involvement in one of the most spectacular shunts ever witnessed at the track, Jim survived unscathed, although a precautionary trip to Methodist Hospital was made for X-rays on his previously injured legs. He would later say he had his eyes closed and had no idea the car had left the ground. Bobby Rahal remembers it as "one of the more memorable moments at Indy." Later in the month, Jim attended a ceremony where he was presented with his Wings of Gold by the US Navy. After his latest major episode in Turn One, Jim was asked what the problem was with that particular corner. "'Well,' Crawford began, furrowing his brow to appear serious, 'there's this blonde that sits about four rows up... I just can't concentrate.'" The crash was the talk of Gasoline Alley. Later in the month it would lead to an unusual announcement. "USAC official Bill Marvel comes into the Star room to announce that to date, there have been 20,000 miles of practice run at the Speedway – then adds that Crawford is the only driver with frequent flier miles."

Jim eventually qualified the back-up car on May 19th, after a hairy four-lap run which averaged 212.200mph, but even that wasn't straightforward. Earlier in the day it had bottomed out again, this time exiting Turn Two. Fortunately, a spin into the infield grass was the result, with nothing more than a damaged nosecone. Jim would start on the penultimate row of the grid in 29th position. "It wasn't for the pole, but it felt like it," said Jim. "Today's been a massive drama. Handling has been our struggle all month. We all know the Buick is potent, but it doesn't do much good if you can't get through the corners." Veteran driver Herm Johnson was working in public relations for the Menard team. Johnson had suffered a career-ending crash at Indianapolis in 1986. "He [Jim] suffered injuries worse than myself. He's just working on courage."

In the race itself, Jim drove doggedly, making the best of a bad situation. He found himself a lap down to Emerson Fittipaldi after less than 25 miles. After such an eventful build-up Jim had an utterly forgettable afternoon in his ill-handling mount. In total he spent almost three and a half minutes in the pits and finished some 17 laps behind the winner, Arie Luyendyk, but it was good enough for 15th place and $130,022.

Chapter Thirteen

Back with Bernstein

" I don't think you become a Hoosier. You are one or you're not. My son, Jeffrey, who'll be three next month, is definitely a Hoosier. He was born at the IU Med Center. He's already talking like a Hoosier."

Back home in Florida, Jim had acquired a new boat. It was a very substantial 52-foot hatteras, complete with tuna tower. Its name? Showing perverse humour, Jim christened the vessel *Turn One*, after the scene of his most serious crash. Jim was never one to forget old friends, and came to the assistance of Paddy Atkinson, his sailing buddy from Belmont. Atkinson approached Jim for some help with a boat in the UK. "Myself and a friend fancied buying quite a big boat, but we were strapped for cash. Jim was doing quite well in the States at the time. 'How short are you? I'll take a share of it.'" With Jim's help the boat was purchased. "He only sailed on it once," remembers Atkinson. "We had a race at Windermere. He came straight from a party, and woke up halfway there. Instead of letting him sleep down below we made him steer the boat, and we won!"

George Roux had first met Jim in 1987, when Jim and Sheila moved to St Petersburg. Roux was an experienced captain and ran fishing charters. The two men quickly became firm friends. "Jim and I immediately hit it off. We shared a rather dry sense of humour."

Jim had been talked into buying *Turn One* by another local captain who persuaded him there was money to be made from fishing charters. The vessel cost in the region of $500,000. Jim soon realised that he had followed bad advice, only undertaking a handful of charters in the first six months. When the other captain was unavailable to take a charter he asked Roux to deputise. "I explained to Jim that the business model proposed to him by his original captain was utter fantasy, and that the boat would never come close to breaking even. He dismissed the original captain and hired me."

Jim would sometimes head out with Roux for a private

> ## I always liked Jim. He was so funny when you sat and talked to him

excursion. "We took a lot of his friends out for fishing and cruising, and had a few trips to the Dry Tortugas and Key West. On one occasion we went on a fishing trip to the Florida Keys. Sheila had this cousin with her. He was scared to death of water. Jim and I had to put up with him for a week." On another occasion Jim treated an elderly relative to an outing, which went spectacularly wrong, as Roux remembers:

"An old aunt of his came out on the boat one time. I decided to make a sudden turn in order to take a shortcut and save us some time. I asked Jim to make sure everyone was aware and secure. Unknown to us the old lady was in the forward rest room. She came bouncing off the pan and slid along the corridor."

Kenny Bernstein returned as an entrant at Indianapolis for 1991 and, naturally, chose Jim as his preferred driver. Throughout the Autumn of 1990 Jim had pounded around the Speedway in a modified Lola. For the race itself he would have a brand-new Lola T91, specifically designed to house the Buick V6 (previous cars had always had to be modified). Jim was back out on track in March 1991, creating headlines with a lap of 224mph, easily the fastest of anyone. Bruce Ashmore, Lola's chief designer, was a big fan. "I always liked Jim. He was so funny when you sat and talked to him, with such a great attitude to life."

The early days of practice at the Speedway were blighted by rain and weepers, with Jim unable to show the true potential of the King Motorsports entry until May 8th, when he turned a lap at over 225mph. He would spend the month swapping between his race and spare car. As usual, it would be a far from straightforward build-up to race day.

Before his 225mph lap Jim had struggled to replicate

An advertising brochure for Turn One. Jim was many things, but he wasn't a businessman. **George Roux**

In his downtime Jim was only too happy to help at charity events.
Author's collection

Jim changed his helmet colours for 1991 to complement the livery of the Quaker State Lolas. **Author's collection**

Jim with his wife, Sheila and the Quaker State Racing team. **Author's collection**

his testing speed. Multiple exhaust and wastegate changes failed to solve the problem. Eventually the team changed springs in the wastegate. Jim described how "the car responded beautifully, and everybody breathed a sigh of relief." Despite this, Jim's woes were far from over. During morning practice on Pole Day he suffered with misfires on both cars, although the team eventually rectified them for a qualifying attempt. He was expected to be near the top of the timesheets, so it was a hugely disappointing run. The four laps (220.2, 220.8, 218.8, 215.8) resulted in an average speed of just 218.947mph. Jim had pushed hard for the first half of his attempt, but the Lola was proving a handful. "The car was getting loose and nearly got away from me two or three times – and that was enough."

Upon his return to the pits, the mystery of the evil handling car was soon solved. A mechanic had mistakenly filled the fuel tank almost to capacity, instead of the small amount needed for qualifying. This, combined with the car's other issues, made Jim's four-lap effort highly commendable. Jim's mood after qualifying was one of frustration. "We've had trouble with the wastegates and the boost, and it fluctuates over three, four, five inches of boost, which is a lot of power. We don't know why. You're out there and it will go fast one minute and slow the next. So, we've got a problem we're gonna have to solve for race day."

Race day was overcast, with a wet track delaying the start by two hours. Pre-race news was dominated by the presence at the track of General Norman Schwarzkopf, and driver Willy T Ribbs, who was about to become the first African American to participate in the Indianapolis 500. Ribbs would strike up a friendship with Jim, who was

never one to keep information from a rookie which could help them. "He was very accommodating. If you asked him about something he would tell you, and he'd spend time with you. He would give you the reason he was telling you it as well."

When the race eventually got underway Jim ran 10th early on, before finally ceding the place to Emerson Fittipaldi's Penske. Jim made his first pit stop on lap 20 for fuel and tyres, but was back just three laps later for a wing and brake adjustment. Now two laps down, he struggled on with his sick sounding mount, only to return to the pitlane for good on lap 43, a victim of electrical gremlins. Jim was classified a forgettable 26th.

In July, 1991, Jim was a special guest at the Pittsburgh Vintage Grand Prix, where he signed autographs and chatted to fans in a Buick hospitality tent. His appearance was so well received that he would return in 1992, as 'Guest of Honor' at the fundraising event. "It's a pleasure to be associated with such a worthwhile effort as raising funds to help the autistic and handicapped children in the Pittsburgh area. I'm pleased that our interest in vintage cars offers a positive effect on the lives of these kids." Also present was legendary French pre-war driver René Dreyfus, as Vintage Driver Emeritus. Conversation between the two must have been fascinating. Jim may or may not have realised the link between Pittsburgh and his place of birth. Andrew Carnegie emigrated from Dunfermline to Pittsburgh during the mid-nineteenth century, where he eventually made his vast fortune in the steel industry. As in Dunfermline, he funded the construction of several public buildings in Pittsburgh, including museums still open today.

*Being interviewed –
Jim was always good
for a quote. Author's
collection*

Chapter Fourteen

233.433

*Jim was all smiles at the Speedway in 1992. **Author's collection***

The 1991 season may have been ultimately disappointing, but the package had obvious potential. Unseasonably cool weather turned the 1992 Indianapolis 500 into an accident filled race. Jim was retained by Bernstein, this time in a Buick powered Lola T92/00, again sponsored by Quaker State. His team-mate for the month of May was the immensely likeable Colombian Roberto Guerrero. Despite being a decade younger, Guerrero was an experienced hand. Like Jim he had raced extensively in Europe (including 29 Formula 1 appearances for the Ensign and Theodore teams) before moving to the US. Guerrero made his CART debut in 1984 – the same year as Jim – and was named Rookie of the Year.

In his first four outings at Indianapolis, Guerrero didn't finish any lower than fourth. He tasted success at the Speedway, but he also experienced disaster. In 1987 he looked a favourite to win the race, only for tragedy to intervene. Tony Bettenhausen's car lost a wheel which rolled into Guerrero's path. Powerless to avoid it, Guerrero's March struck the errant wheel with terrific force, catapulting it up and over the safety fence. Unfortunately, the wheel landed on a grandstand, killing 41-year-old spectator Lyle Kurtenbach. Guerrero himself came close

to losing his life at the Speedway later the same year. A few months after Jim's 1987 Indy shunt, Guerrero was testing at the circuit and suffered an enormous accident which left him in a coma for 17 days.

Although the two men did not socialise together their similarly laid-back personas made them ideal team-mates. They had previously raced against each other in Europe, as Guerrero remembers. "Jim and I knew each other during the F2 and European seasons but got to know each other much better when we were team-mates at Indy." Both were thrilled to be driving cars which quickly emerged as the class of the field. During testing in late March Guerrero became the first driver ever to lap the speedway at an average speed of over 230mph. Jim quickly matched the feat and confidence in the team was high when official practice got underway on Saturday, May 2nd.

Jim couldn't get over 230mph on the opening day, but still topped the timesheets with a lap of 229.609mph. The following day saw Guerrero finally crack the magic figure with a lap of 230.432mph. Not to be outdone Jim headed out the next day. With the aid of a tow from Scott Brayton Jim lapped the Brickyard at over 232mph, but this was not good enough in his eyes. On a subsequent lap without a tow Jim

*Thundering around the speedway on his way to setting record speeds. **Author's collection***

The Lola-Buick combination was quick throughout the month of May, but luck deserted both Jim and his team-mate. **Author's collection**

recorded an incredible average speed of 233.433 mph. He subsequently explained why he had gone out again. "I dropped back so I could hardly see the guy in front of me. That was more enjoyable. We can forget the one with the tow. I didn't want to go to sleep with everyone saying I did it with a tow."

Guerrero was also lapping easily above 230mph, while no other drivers had yet come close to matching the Quaker State pair. Even with a new unofficial lap record to his name Jim was typically gracious and refused to accept all the credit. "I've learned a lot by looking at Roberto's computer tracers. I'm learning ways around the corners I've never thought of and it's paying off."

Undoubtedly the two drivers worked well together, but Jim was perhaps underplaying his contribution. He was greatly valued as a test driver and for his ability to set up cars, as Bernstein was only too aware. "Jim was excellent in setting up a race car. He had a tremendous feel for the race car. Jim was a prince of a person. He was one of the easiest drivers to work with in any form of racing. He always gave you everything he had."

Lola designer Bruce Ashmore goes into more detail about Jim's vital role in developing the 1992 car. It shows the remarkable ability Jim had for both driving and analysing exactly what a car was doing:

"The Buick had always had the power, but it would never qualify on pole. I wanted to understand why. I sat and talked to Jim one morning, because Mark Scott had told me that Jim had done the most miles with it around the Speedway. Jim said he would go into a corner and have to lift, because there was too much power. With the 2.6-litre engines you could go flat if you ran enough wing angle, but with the 3.5-litre Buick – even if you ran maximum wing – you couldn't get it flat, and it would just understeer anyway because you couldn't balance that amount of rear wing. Jim told me he would lift and then, when he got back on the power, he could feel the rear wheels spin slightly and then lose rear grip. The car would oversteer, so he would lift again to stop the rear sliding out. Then he would get back on the power, but by then the car would understeer all the way to the exit of the corner. He told me that, if he could keep the throttle down when he had the rear-wheel spin phase, he was sure that he and the other Buick drivers could balance it all the way to the exit.

"I thought, if I moved the weight forward on the Buick car, then that would make the understeer happen more from the lateral load and less from the power understeer, and could give him the balance he was looking for. This was one of those 'Aha!' moments in my career, when you sat and talked to a driver and got the understanding of the feeling they had when they were in that zone on the track. This happens very

The Lola had to be in line for qualifying by noon or Jim's hopes of pole would be gone

rarely, with very few drivers, and it means so much to a designer because you want to know these things, but we can never do the physical driving part ourselves. The really clever part is Jim could do that and relay it in words to me. Only the great drivers can. Drivers like Mario Andretti had this ability, and I spent most of my time with him over the years. With the new information from Jim I went back to England and designed the 1992 series of cars. One for the standard engines [Chevrolet-Ilmor, Cosworth DFS and Alfa Romeo], one for the new Ford Cosworth XB, and finally a car especially for the Buick V6. I moved the rear wheels back a full three inches, with a longer bellhousing. Then I did an aero programme dedicated to this part of the Indycar project. I figured that, with all the extra power we had, the aero kit didn't need to be as efficient as for the other engines. The Buick would always have too much power to go flat all the way round, and so more downforce would definitely help, and the associated extra drag wouldn't hurt too much. The car came out of the box flying. John Travis was the engineer I put on this project, and he came up with the unique set-up that the car needed to squeeze the last piece of performance out of it."

Willy T Ribbs has his own opinion on why Jim was so well respected by Buick, and used for the bulk of the development work. "Buick knew he had the testosterone to run that son of a bitch!" Running consistently quick laps on the intimidating superspeedways required a certain skill set, which Jim undoubtedly had. Gordon Kirby describes the delicate balancing act. "You have to be aggressive, but not too aggressive. Smooth and fast, but precise." The Quaker State team-mates were thoroughly enjoying themselves, with Bernstein denying there was inter-team rivalry between the pair. Jim had his own thoughts on the subject. "Oh, yes there is... We're race car drivers for God's sake... But it's all in good fun."

May 6th and 7th saw further practice, and two huge crashes. Four-time Indy winner Rick Mears was fortunate to escape with light injuries when his Penske crashed on its own oil and flipped over. Formula One refugee Nelson Piquet was not so fortunate the following day. The Brazilian three-time World Champion spun his Menard entered Lola in Turn Four and impacted the retaining wall with sickening force head on. Piquet suffered serious leg injuries and would spend many months recuperating. One of his visitors at Methodist Hospital was his team-mate, Gary Bettenhausen. The pair had struck up an unlikely close friendship while working together. Piquet, the globetrotting, multi-millionaire grand prix superstar, and Bettenhausen, the seasoned old pro who was a veteran of America's tough and dangerous sprint car scene.

On May 8th Mario Andretti and Arie Luyendyk finally managed to creep above 230 mph, with the former recording an impressive lap of 233.202mph. Next up was Pole Day and it looked set up for an epic battle as drivers sought to eke out every ounce of performance to complete their four consecutive timed laps in the shortest possible time. Although the Quaker State cars were expected to dominate Pole Day proceedings Jim was still wary. "I think the most foolish thing to do would be to sit back and say we've done it." Despite his outwardly laid-back appearance, Jim took Indianapolis very seriously indeed. Three months before the event each year he went on a strict diet and stopped drinking alcohol. He also realised the chance afforded him and strove to repay the faith put in him by the team. Every evening both drivers would stay until 8pm or later in technical debriefs, intent on maximising every possible aspect of their equipment. Jim had great respect for Bernstein and the crew he had assembled. "Attitude is what it comes down to, the whole King Motorsports organisation. We want for nothing. If it's out there, we've got it. And it's showing in the results – a first-rate effort that comes from the top."

May 9th began with a practice session and Jim suffered a setback almost immediately, when a blown Buick V6 caused him to spin. While Guerrero recorded a four-lap run late in the day at an average of 232.482mph the King Racing mechanics worked furiously to install a new engine in Jim's car. They were in luck, as the session ran behind schedule and necessitated Pole Day being carried over into the Sunday.

The pole looked certain to go to one of the Quaker State cars. The only question was whether Jim could dislodge his team-mate from the top spot. If he could, he would be $100,000 better off, the amount being offered to the fastest driver by CART series sponsors PPG. Once again, Jim headed out for morning practice and once again – in an incredibly cruel twist of fate – his engine failed. The green and white car was towed back to the pits where Jim's mechanics swarmed over it. They had considerably less than an hour to effect an engine change. The Lola had to be in line for qualifying by noon or Jim's hopes of pole would be gone. The Quaker State crew performed little short of a miracle by installing a new Buick in 48 minutes, but it wasn't quick enough. Fate had once again dealt Jim a cruel and frustrating blow. Immediately afterwards he was interviewed by Jack Arute and was remarkably circumspect about losing the opportunity of a lifetime. Perhaps, given his history at the speedway, he had come to expect such things:

Jack: "Jim, you came close. You blew an engine in the last practice session, and you guys just thrashed at it, but you didn't make it in time for first day qualifying:

Jim: "No, I think we missed it by six minutes there. It was a helluva try though, 40 minutes for an engine change."

Jack: "But on the way up they were still working on the car."

Once again Jim suffered a disappointing race day, and another year passed without the success his dedication to Indianapolis deserved. **Author's collection**

Jim: "Yeah... The rule book says we've got to be there when called for. So, eh, we just tried it. We brought it out in bits and thought we could maybe carry on building it in the line here. But they said no, so we'll go and finish it properly and just take a second-day deal."

They did finish it properly, and Jim headed out later the same day to set the sixth fastest time of 228.859mph. Due to his failure to set the time during the pole session, however, he would start the race in a lowly 21st position. This placed Jim on row eight alongside Al Unser and AJ Foyt, both four-time winners of the 500. It led to one of Jim's great quips, when interviewed by Dr Jerry Punch about his position alongside the two legends. "Between us, we've won it eight times. So, I think we're looking good." His quick wittedness brought hilarity in the ESPN commentary booth shared by Dave Despain and Derek Daly.

In an interview for this book Guerrero gave his thoughts on Jim's failure to make pole day. "I don't remember exactly what we talked about, but it was a shame because we could have been 1-2. It would have been fun." Guerrero's run was good enough for pole, and the $100,000 cheque that came with it. Jim was gracious in losing his chance to challenge. "If it had to be anybody, I'm glad it was my team-mate."

Later, Jim would reflect on his failure to get a shot at pole. "They've worked hard, every day, every night. Then to see it slip away through no fault of their own is equally as tragic for them as it is for me. It's a team game and we all felt terrible, terrible... what's a worse word than terrible?"

Quaker State crewman Mike Perkins was one of those who desperately tried to get Jim's car to the qualifying line in time. It was a painful experience, as a Speedway safety worker bumped into him causing Perkins to stumble and fall, where he was run over by one of the Lola's wheels. Jim was suitably impressed by his mechanic's acrobatics, noting that, "...instead of falling on the car, on the wing, he decided to fall under it, which I thought was pretty noble."

Following Jim's successful qualifying run Bernstein opted to sell his back-up car to Dale Coyne. Rookie Brian Bonner would go on to qualify it in 26th position at over 220 mph, only to crash out shortly before half distance.

With two weeks still to go until race day there were still plenty of drivers desperate to qualify. One of the most impressive rookies at the speedway in 1992 was the Filipino driver Jovy Marcelo, who was driving for the Euromotorsport team. Shortly after 4pm on May 15th Marcelo lost control in Turn One and spun into the wall on his first flying lap of the day. He suffered a basal skull fracture and was pronounced dead a short time later. Marcelo was 27 years old and the first driver to die at Indianapolis since Gordon Smiley crashed fatally during qualifying for the 1982 event (coincidentally also on May 15th). His loss was keenly felt in the close-knit community of Gasoline Alley. Despite being a rookie, Marcelo had quickly been accepted into the Indianapolis fold. He left a five-year-old son, and his wife who was expecting their second child.

On a positive note, Indianapolis veteran and legend Tom Sneva finally managed to land a drive for the big race, which he had won in 1983. Sneva had to be tracked down on the golf course to be informed that his services were required by John Menard, after Rocky Moran proved too tall to fit into one of the team's Lolas. Sneva grabbed the opportunity, but was somewhat unprepared as Tim Considine noticed during a press conference. "I ask him what is under the name patch on his obviously borrowed fire suit. 'Jim Crawford, and he needs to lose some weight'."

Despite being safely in the field, Jim was at the track for Bump Day, watching the action from the pitwall. He was keen to see some bumping take place, which – due to the 500's complex qualifying format – could potentially move him forward a few places in the starting line-up. Shortly

before the six o'clock gun to signal the end of qualifying rookie Ted Prappas made the field, and Jim found himself promoted to the outside of row seven. With Jim's practice speeds throughout May his prospects looked good for the race. Even Roger Penske considered the Quaker State cars a threat. "I can tell you that if Guerrero and Crawford... can run the speeds all day long they're gonna be tough to beat."

Race day was unusually cold for late May. Jim and the rest of the 33-driver field knew that generating and maintaining tyre temperature would be crucial. As the pace car led the field around on the warm-up laps, Guerrero also had tyre temperature on his mind in the pole-sitting Quaker State car. While trying to generate some heat on Indy's back stretch the car snapped sideways, skittering across the infield grass and nudging the inside retaining wall. Despite the low speed at which the accident occurred Guerrero was out on the spot. It was a heart-breaking end for the Colombian who had finished second on two previous occasions at the Speedway. Guerrero wasn't the only driver to be caught out by the cold track before the race started. Frenchman Philippe Gache spun his Dick Simon-entered car in Turn One, but was able to rejoin.

With Guerrero's demise King Racing's hopes now lay solely with Jim, but he was stuck far down the field. By lap 74 Jim was still in the running, with Rick Mears in the Penske close behind. While negotiating Turn One, Jim's car lost adhesion and slid sideways towards the wall. Mears, with nowhere to go, slammed into Jim's car. Moments later Emerson Fittipaldi, in the other Penske, also lost control in Turn One, leaving three wrecked cars to be cleared away.

For the King team it was a bitterly disappointing end to a race that had promised so much, with both cars out well before half distance. Despite this, Guerrero still holds fond memories of his 1992 Indianapolis 500 experience. "That car was awesome, especially the way we were able to set it up. It was great having such a superior car and team that year."

The rest of the race featured several other frightening accidents, which saw Methodist Hospital busier than usual with battered racing drivers. To give an idea of the carnage that day the following is a list of drivers who crashed out: Roberto Guerrero, Tom Sneva, Philippe Gache, Stan Fox, Rick Mears, Jim Crawford, Emerson Fittipaldi, Mario Andretti, Jimmy Vasser, Brian Bonner, Jeff Andretti, Gary Bettenhausen and Arie Luyendyk. Jim could see the comedy in any situation, as Tim Considine noted in 1992's *The Indianapolis 500 Yearbook*:

"Funniest post-race statement – Crawford, who else, after returning from the hospital on this brutal day: "Methodist Hospital is like the Hall of Fame. Nurses kept pointing, 'There's Rick Mears, there's Emerson Fittipaldi, there's Tom Sneva.' Let's see, including Mario Andretti and Nelson Piquet – that's seven Indy 500 wins and six Formula One World Championships in one hospital at the same time!"

Chapter Fifteen

Last Time Out

After the record speeds of 1992, slowing the cars down became a priority for 1993. The track was narrowed, which clearly had the desired effect, as Jim noted. "As you all know, there's a new grassy area where I used to run. We usually came in with 10 to 15 days of testing behind us and learning the new track has been... interesting. The hardest part is that you can't drive round it, you just sit there and aim it. You're not driving, you're aiming, whereas before you could modify your line and stay with the throttle. Now you can't adapt or adjust."

The favoured racing line of Jim's, below the white line at the apex of the corners, had been grassed over. Derek Daly commented on how it disadvantaged Jim during qualifying. "That's the line they took away from Jim Crawford... Jim's favourite line has now gone, and that has caused him a tremendous amount of problems... That's where Jim needs to be, and likes to be and wants to be."

Willy T Ribbs was back in 1993, and found the changes made a significant difference, making the track trickier to negotiate. "It made your corner entry more important. Especially Turn One, because you couldn't see that corner. I'm talking about split second timing, or you could have yourself a problem." The 1986 Indianapolis 500 winner Bobby Rahal also found the changes a challenge. "It narrowed the circuit considerably. Everybody used the apron in the race. You would go down there to keep out of the turbulence of the car ahead."

By the time the track opened for practice in 1993, Jim and Sheila had become parents to a second child. Emily Crawford was born on March 12th. The King Motorsports Lolas carried Budweiser sponsorship, with Indycar legend Al Unser joining Guerrero and Jim for a three-car assault. For the first time since 1984 Jim would not have Buick power behind him, with the team running Chevrolets instead. All three drivers tested at the Speedway during April, and early indications were that the track modifications would result in significantly slower lap times.

Guerrero got to sample Jim's number 60 Lola two days before Jim had his first run in it. Early practice saw Jim topping 219mph, while Guerrero managed

Jim's last 500 in 1993. **Jim Knerr**

more than 224mph. The Colombian successfully qualified on Pole Day, but both Jim and Al Unser had their attempts waved off. Unser made the field the next day, but Jim would have to sweat until the next weekend. He was clearly not happy with the situation. "It's been a bit frustrating, trying to run three cars, and it's quite obvious that Roberto and I can't share set-ups...

He runs in very smooth and drives with the throttle. I start trying to go in harder, overload the right front and it gives out. I needed to build up my confidence because I've been stuck at 217 to 218 and scaring myself. The car's way ahead of me at the moment... there's more in it, maybe 224 to 225."

By the time his next opportunity came he had turned a lap at over 221mph, using Unser's engine. The rules forbade an engine from being used to qualify more than one car, so the team had a new motor flown in. Typical of Jim's luck at the Speedway, the airline dropped and broke it, necessitating yet another to be sent. It arrived in time, and Jim used it to qualify with a 217.612mph four-lap average. It was good enough to secure a start, albeit way down in 31st position.

On the grid come race day, Jim didn't get away with the rest of the field. The car eventually did fire up, after a tense few seconds. His race was seriously compromised early on when he lost the Lola in Turn Two, miraculously spinning without hitting anything. A pitstop followed to replace flat-spotted tyres but the car was never on the pace for the rest of the day. Jim soldiered on regardless to a forgettable 24th place finish, eight laps down on Emerson Fittipaldi's winning Penske. It was still good enough to win just under $150,000 in prize money and he had a better day than Guerrero, who crashed out with Jeff Andretti.

Bruce Ashmore laments the switch from Buick to Chevrolet power in 1993. "In 1992, if the weather had been different, the Buicks would have been in contention for the win all day. John [Travis] and the drivers were broken up from the Buick project in 1993. It was a shame, because if someone had entered it again with that team of guys, as they did the previous year, that combination would have been the one to beat. Jim really understood how to get the most out of the Buick power."

> ### Jim's favourite line has now gone, and that has caused him a tremendous amount of problems

One of the last images of Jim lapping Indianapolis. The dream was almost over. **Indianapolis Motor Speedway**

Jim had raced for the final time at Indianapolis. His two further appearances in 1994 and 1995 would be but footnotes in 500 history. Saddled with hopelessly outclassed older cars he didn't even attempt to qualify. Mark Scott and Bob Riley did what they could with a modified 1991 Lola in 1994. They felt Jim missing out on the Month of May just didn't seem right, as the former related. "We've got no sponsors. It's just Riley and me. We couldn't let a guy like Jim Crawford go without a ride here."

Jim was appreciative of their efforts. "The only reason I've committed to an old car is because I have a lot of

Mark Scott (second from right) did all he could to give his friend a ride for the 500 in 1994, but the car was never going to qualify. **Mark Scott**

confidence in those two guys." Bob Riley worked hard to improve the car's suspension, and Jim Wright loaned an engine to be used for testing. While busy building Trans-Am cars for customers, the Indy effort was only costing money, as Scott noted. "We're further down the food chain than we've been before, so we're running this thing out of our pockets."

The 1991 Lola, conspicuously devoid of advertising, could not be coaxed past 218.5mph and rising track temperatures saw Jim turn a lap of just 211.4. It certainly wasn't for lack of effort, remembers Scott. "He was trying as hard as he could, and I think the lack of grip scared him once or twice, but we were all involved in the decision to withdraw. We all knew that the limiting factor was the old car. Once we'd withdrawn, Jim hung out with us at the garage and generally enjoyed himself." Jim was his usual realistic and magnaminous self. "We were lacking a bit of downforce compared with the newer cars and, with the heat, it was a pretty much impossible task."

Willy T Ribbs was a great admirer of Jim's bravery at the Speedway. "He could carry his testicles in a wheelbarrow, the way he hung it out around Indy. In 1990, when he broke the altitude record, the car was very unstable. An '89 Lola with diffusers. All the other drivers who drove one came back in looking like deer in the headlights. He was badass."

Rumours persisted that Jim had been offered a seat in more than one other car at the Speedway that month. He didn't deny it, but neither did he ever contemplate accepting

In contemplative mood. The speed and determination was still there, but Jim's injuries and health issues were beginning to catch him up.
Author's collection

any of them. "As I look at it, it's a team sport. I'd hate to be dumped by a team in the middle of the month, so why should I do it to them?"

Jeff Shuttleworth visited his cousin several times in Florida, and enjoyed being in Jim's company away from the stresses of racing. "He took me out on the boat, just drinking and cruising. We stopped at a pub on the coast on the other side from Jim's house, and he was pointing places out to me. 'That's Hulk Hogan's house, and that's Nigel Mansell's house. We'll wave at Nige.' Then he asked if I could go down below and press a certain button on a panel. When I did there was a huge horn sound and he informed me I'd just dumped the lavatory."

Jim made a final attempt to qualify for the 500 in 1995, driving for Gerald Adcox, a car importer from Pensacola, Florida. Adcox fielded both Lola and Reynard chassis. The Lola had been owned by Ron Hemelgarn. A deal was made with Adcox, as Hemelgarn remembers. "Gerald dealt in exotic cars. I traded him that racecar for a Ford GT40, '67 Mustang convertible and '68 GT500. I still have the cars. Another team wanted to give me a piece of real estate for it, but I said 'Give me those cars!'" Jim tried both the Lola and Reynard, but spent most of his time trying to get the latter up to speed. It was a 1994 Reynard 94I, with Ford power. Parts for the model were scarce, which seriously disrupted the team's practice schedule. After days fruitlessly searching for an anti-roll bar they had to fabricate one themselves. When the car finally made it out it blew an engine. Meanwhile, Jim saw his unofficial track record of 233.433mph finally broken, having stood since 1992. Dutchman Arie Luyendyk ticked off a lap at 234.107mph. Jim was asked by Dick Denny of *The Indianapolis News* if

> It's tougher this year. There's better cars, but I've got a better driver. I've got the best driver for this car.

he was surprised. "No, I'm surprised it lasted as long as it did." He was, however, quick to point out that he still held one claim to fame at the Speedway. "I still hold the altitude record here in my famous flying car."

As Jim sat on the sidelines watching his competitors get up to speed, he began to cling to hope more than reality with regards to making the race. "If I had to, I'd come back and watch the race, but I don't want to pull out. Why would you do that? I think 224 should do it, and I think there's one in it. The tyres are better this year. We're going to run on Firestones."

When Jim did finally make it on track for some laps he could ignore reality no longer. He managed to coax a lap at a shade over 218mph from the Lola, while the Reynard seemed stuck in the 217mph bracket. Jim damned the Lola with faint praise. "The car isn't actually that bad. It's just slow. That's the worst kind to have." Adcox remained upbeat about their chances, and never doubted Jim's abilities. "It's tougher this year. There's better cars, but I've got a better driver. I've got the best driver for this car."

Jim must have known that his chances of getting the car above the 225mph needed to qualify were virtually nil, and in the end no attempt was made. Even amid his own disappointment and frustrations Jim found time congratulate previous employer, John Menard, who secured first and second starting positions. "He's put a lot of money in this and his goal is to stick a couple of cars on the front row and blitz the record. Good for him. John deserves it."

Derek Daly was sorry to see Jim's final, unsuccessful attempts at the Speedway. "He became an Indy specialist. This was both good and bad. It was good because his bravery – which was still there after the accident – caused people to put him back in a car at Indy, but there is no way a driver is really ready to be competitive when he only does Indy each year. At this stage of his career, Jim was just racing at Indy to make money."

Scott believes he did harbour hopes of returning to Indianapolis and racing again. "I think he did want to go back, though he was in a lot of pain and realised he had to have that addressed first." Never being able to compete in the event which had become – out of necessity – the focal point of his life, must have been a truly depressing reality for Jim. In 1993, the last year he made the race, he made his feelings clear. "I just love it here. Old friends. Old faces. Love it."

Derek Daly thinks taking the Indianapolis 500 away from Jim played a significant role in how the remaining years of his life played out. "He was quiet, shy, brave, unfulfilled. After his accident there was a huge void in Jim's life that was never filled. This void began his tailspin because Jim did not appear to have anything in his life but motor racing."

The fans loved an underdog, and Jim was in high demand for autographs and pictures right until the very end. **Author's collection**

*Getting ready for battle in 1993. It would be the final time Jim made the field for his beloved 500. **Author's collection***

Chapter Sixteen

Time Running Out

Getting a bite, and enjoying a beer on Turn One with good friend and fellow racer, Gary Bettenhausen. **Boardman family**

Following his final attempt at Indy in 1995, Jim returned to Tierra Verde and his beloved boat. His house contained some reminders of his career. He possessed the steering wheel from that fateful day in 1987, presented to him by his mechanics. Bent like a pretzel it was displayed with a brass plaque below which read, 'The fastest man ever into Turn One.' While much of his time was spent fishing Jim also used the boat for occasional charters and indulged other interests. In his 40s he learned to dive, along with his friend and neighbour Phil Smithies, who also hailed from Lancashire. Smithies had originally met Jim in the mid-1980s when he owned the Dresser's Arms pub near Bolton. Smithies subsequently ran an Italian restaurant on the A675, where pride of place on the wall was given to a large lithograph of Jim at Indianapolis in his Lola-Buick. He emigrated to America where he opened a restaurant in St Petersburg and started a non-profit organisation to help disabled sailors. Smithies himself had at one time been a competitor in the dangerous world of motorcycle road racing.

In Florida he soon regretted having Jim as a diving partner, when he discovered his friend's approach to buddy breathing. This technique requires divers to share an oxygen supply in the event that the other person's fails. "The instructor – an English guy – turned Jim's air off first. I handed him my mouthpiece, which he bit and wouldn't let go of. When my air was turned off he didn't give me his mouthpiece at all. The instructor was in hysterics and I had no option but to return to the surface. Fortunately it was only a five-metre deep swimming pool."

Jim's marriage to Sheila eventually failed and in the aftermath he relocated to nearby Tierra Verde, where he moved into a condo. George Roux lived in the same complex at the time following his own divorce. "We called the place 'Heartbreak Hotel'." Jim enjoyed using his boat for bar hopping along the Florida coast. His most frequent haunt

was Smuggler's Tavern in Tierra Verde, where Roux recalls he was "something of a fixture." One evening spent at the Smuggler's sticks in Roux's mind:

"Jim had a bit too much to drink and I offered him a lift home. He'd just bought the condo and there must have been a hundred identical ones. Well, we're driving past them and I'm asking him which one is his. 'I don't know George, I don't know.' All I can think about is getting arrested for prowling up and down. It was two or three in the morning. I asked him, 'Does this look like it?' 'They all look the same.' Then, 'Wait. I might recognise the flower I put out the front.' Just when the situation seemed hopeless Jim piped up. 'There's one thing that might work.' He fumbled around and pulled out a key fob which he started pressing. Eventually a garage door started opening. 'That's mine!'"

It was in Florida that Jim met Annie, a striking blonde who he fell for immediately. In 1998 the couple were married in a simple backyard ceremony in Tierra Verde. Jim had upgraded to a larger condo by this time, a short distance away. In his home he kept a collection of tropical fish, another of his interests. Traces of his previous life could also be found. They included one of his old crash helmets, which he had made into a novelty telephone. Unable to race any longer, Jim entered fishing tournaments to satisfy his competitive urge.

Jim didn't leave motor racing behind completely. He carried out some consultancy work for the American racing car manufacturer Riley & Scott (which his close friend Mark Scott was a partner in) and also worked for them as a driver coach. He also acted as a spotter for his old friend John Menard's team at Indy. Former rival Derek Daly recalled meeting Jim while working as a commentator for Speed channel:

"I was at Texas Motor Speedway to do the TV broadcast when I went up into the grandstands during practice to watch. Sitting by himself also watching was Jim. I went over to speak to him and he told me that one of his injured legs had healed badly. His leg and ankle had grown together at a severe angle. He sounded depressed because he did not have the money to have corrective surgery and his insurance had run out. I felt sorry for Jim and I went to Championship Auto Racing Auxiliary (CARA – a drivers' wives association which raised money for charities) and suggested that they consider Jim as a driver who needed their support. CARA provided the funding for Jim to have what may have been his last surgery."

David Chapman also helped Jim out in his final years, at the suggestion of the late, legendary racing journalist Robin Miller. "I'd just started my open-wheel oval racing school in Lakeland, Florida. I got a 'phone call from Robin in Indianapolis. Would I consider helping a friend of his who was a bit down on his luck? 'Of course,' I said. Robin then told me about Jim. There were days when he could barely walk, but Robin thought he would make a great instructor. It was during our first get together at the track that Jim made an unforgettable comment – 'Just tell 'em, don't turn right!'"

Jim, who had never possessed the financial means to attend a racing school himself as a youngster, struggled to relate to the concept of teaching students how to become a racing driver. Chapman remembers that "Jim never did commit one way or another. I just don't think he ever saw himself as an instructor. He wasn't a big believer in racing schools, he implied. His attitude was 'You're either talented or you're not, and the only way to learn how to race is to race.' Very old school, but inarguable in many ways.

As Jim's involvement in racing drew to a close, he would have one final influence on the sport he lived for. It is an

> ## You're either talented or you're not, and the only way to learn how to race is to race

episode which has been kept secret for over 20 years, but Chapman now feels the time is right to detail the role Jim played in the career of a future Indianapolis 500 winner:

"I was contacted by a young British driver who was going to be racing in the FF2000 series in America, which would also include some ovals. He'd never driven on an oval, and didn't want to risk his current race car – or embarrass himself in front of the wrong people, he said – in doing a first test. Would we let him do a few laps in our car at Lakeland, just to get a feel for it? I agreed, if it was under supervision. We told Jim that our driver had already achieved some success in the UK and was not a novice, so he agreed to 'supervise'.

"Dan Wheldon arrived arrived at the track around 9am. Jim was a little late arriving, but they seemed to get along well. Few people knew about it, and I have to admit I was reluctant to go ahead because I knew Jon Baytos who ran Primus Racing, Dan's FF2000 team owner. The secrecy agreement stipulated no photographs and no publicity. I never really knew why Dan didn't want Jon to know – I thought he would think it a good idea. After all, we were risking my car, not his. But Dan had his reasons.

"Jim took Dan around the track – a three-quarter mile oval – in a regular road car, and spent some time with him explaining the things he needed to know. They came in and we fitted Dan into our Reynard SF92. In all, he spent around two hours in the car coming in and out of the pits, with Jim watching from different positions around the track. I'm not sure what he told him, but it obviously helped. Of course, we didn't realise how special Dan would turn out to be, so no big deal was made about it. I would give anything to have just one photo. I think Dan thought that, if he did have an

*With second wife, Annie. **Boardman Family***

*Spending time with daughter, Emily. **Boardman Family***

After his own driving career finished Jim still kept in touch with his racing friends, such as Mark Scott pictured here. **Boardman Family**

incident, at least it wouldn't be in front of his team. As for Jim, I think he understood exactly why Dan was doing it

his way. 'Lots of time I wish people hadn't seen my mistakes,' he remarked."

Eventually, Jim sold *Turn One*. "When he finally sold the boat he took a pretty good loss, and had no desire to get another one," Roux remembers. Despite this he remained very much involved in the local maritime scene. Roux worked for Annheuser Busch at their lavish complex on St Petersburg beach which featured luxury facilities and a marina of expensive yachts. Through his friend, Jim was introduced to the people there, becoming a frequent visitor. "He was well liked down there" recalls Roux. "They loved to hear about his racing background."

It was Roux who introduced Jim to fellow Brit Richard Thompson, and his new wife Dena. The couple had recently moved to Florida from the UK, hoping to buy into a sport fishing venture. Jim got on well with the Thompsons, but everything was not as it seemed. After losing touch for a while, Roux was contacted by Richard who told him that Dena had tried to kill him. Eventually it emerged that his new wife was in fact a murderer who had disposed of her previous husband by cooking him a poisoned curry. She was also suspected of having killed another partner and was ultimately exposed as a serial bigamist and defrauder.

Old racing friends occasionally visited Jim in Florida, particularly John Menard, and Gary and Tony Bettenhausen, as Roux recalls. "Jim told me he had some racing buddies coming to visit. I went down to get the boat ready about 5am. While I was busy loading bait I heard a crash in the bushes. It turned out to be the Bettenhausens, returning from a night out in Tampa much the worse for wear."

Although Jim maintained a brave face the truth was that his health was failing. He confided in close friends that he had contracted hepatitis, the result of a contaminated

skin graft in the aftermath of the 1987 Indy crash. Smithies recalls that, despite the often intense pain, his friend, "never bitched and never moaned." Willy T Ribbs was another who admired Jim's resilience. "He never mentioned his injuries. He was old school tough, like AJ [Foyt] and Bobby [Unser]." Roux was a near neighbour of Jim's and could see the deterioration taking place. "He came round one day and said, 'Look at my leg.' It was swollen up to twice normal size and I told him he better get to a doctor. I guess that was the beginning of his liver failing."

David Chapman saw Jim in Florida several times after the day spent coaching Dan Wheldon. "Jim's health began to deteriorate. Subsequent meetings with him were either at the marina or in the bar directly across from his home in Tierra Verde. He had his own barstool reserved, right in front of a whole collection of Crawford memorabilia that the owner was clearly proud to display. I was with Jim in his apartment one day, looking at some cuttings he had in a scrap book. I'm not sure if he made a habit of collecting, but he was obviously very proud of his many accomplishments. I last saw him about a year or so before he died. His health was getting worse, but he was a very funny guy. Unassuming, with a dry wit. Very self-deprecating. One of the things Jim could do very well was laugh at himself. At the end of the day all he ever wanted to do was race. He was, I believe, born of the same mould as Ronnie Peterson, Gilles Villeneuve and Keke Rosberg, et al; those who only knew how to drive foot-to-the-floor fast, all the time – no compromising. He was brave and fearless but, many times, luck just wasn't on his side. When his luck finally did run out the world lost one of its true characters."

Jim returned to Bolton for a holiday with Annie, where he met up with long-time friend Mike Peers. "We went out for dinner. He was a bit of a mess, with his leg swollen up. Afterwards they came back to our house. Now Jim never danced, but we got him up that night. I think there was a feeling in the air, like we all knew, including Jim, that his time was probably limited. He wanted to buy a house in Belmont that he planned to restore, but it didn't happen. He went back to Florida and died not long after." Peers describes Jim as, "a strange, charismatic person and *über*-competitive. Wouldn't put his hand in his pocket though!"

"I think he missed the Bolton crowd" says Janet Donnison. "I remember him calling me one night, it was Rob Moores' birthday. I picked up the phone and he said, 'They are all there, except you and me'."

Jim's body gave up for good on August 6th, 2002. He passed away at his Tierra Verde home at just 54 years old. Mark Scott recalled the last time he saw his old driver and great friend. "I saw him when he came to Indy a couple of weeks before he died. He had hoped to be able to have some more foot surgery, but complications with other organs took away that option. What was interesting was his attitude was almost one of relief. He knew nothing more could be done

Jim never gave less than his all, regardless of the equipment. **Author's collection**

and he had reconciled himself to that fact. The next I knew was a call from Annie saying he'd passed."

Jim's acceptance of his fate was also expressed to Rick Rising-Moore, who ran the Union Jack pub in Indianapolis, a favourite haunt of Jim's. "We had a couple of beers and he said, 'I think I am all in.' He was really hobbling about by that time. After he had his accident I could see the agony in his face."

For Phil Smithies it was tough to watch his friend's health deteriorating. "Jim was definitely in a tailspin. Racing was his life. The diving, the fishing. Nothing could really get him motivated. It was a shame, as we all tried."

Stephen Choularton's life had taken a very different course to that of his old Atlantic team-mate. He emigrated to Australia in 1993 and became involved in organic farming. Having lost touch with Jim many years before, he found out about his death via the internet. "My wife discovered an article on Google. She searched for 'Jim Crawford', just wondering what had happened to him, and read his obituary. When I came home she told me. I had no idea how he had died as it was just referred to as a mysterious disease. What a shame. You do all these dangerous things and then get caught like that."

Bob Fernley was also shocked to hear of Jim's passing. "I only found out through the media and was not aware how ill he had become." Whitney Ganz – Jim's team-mate at Conte Racing during the IMSA days – mourned his death. "He was a great guy and I very much enjoyed the time I spent driving with him. He also gave me one of the greatest compliments I ever got while driving. I was so sorry to hear about his passing. He should have won Indy. He was so close. While we were driving together I considered him a good friend. He was such a nice guy from start to finish. I'll always remember Jim with a big smile. A real competitor, but definitely enjoyed

what he did." Roman Kuzma heard the news by phone. "Somebody called and said, 'You won't believe this. Jim's dead.' It was a shock. He was a very likeable guy. I wish I had kept more in touch, but racing full time is such a time consumer. A sad end indeed, but I will always remember him warmly."

Richard Jones always enjoyed his time in Jim's company. "I don't think I ever raced against Jim, but we were on the same wavelength. Both flying by the seat of our pants! He was great fun when he was on form, but not very good at the politics of the sport. Jim was a stunning, raw talent. He was strong, aggressive and fair. He was technically excellent, and had world champion potential."

Ted Wentz, Jim's old Atlantic sparring partner, also remembers him fondly. "We had quite a few good dices, the outcome of which could go either way. On a personal level I recall Jim as being a decent and unassuming fellow with bushy hair and a broad northern accent. He had a great pool of talent and was a relentless charger. I am glad his career progressed far beyond Formula Atlantic. He didn't descend from wealthy beginnings and won his drives the old-fashioned way. He earned them. For these reasons he had my deep respect. It is a great shame that he isn't with us today."

Rod Lee, a friend from the old days in Bolton, remembers exactly where he was when he heard the news. "I was in the Co-op and I saw Phil Davies. He said, 'I've been trying to call you. Jim died.' He was so easy-going, and never had a bad word about anyone. A good mate, who got on with everybody."

Childhood friend, Janet Donnison, stayed in contact with Jim until the end, even though she hadn't seen him in person since 1982. "Jim and I left the UK that autumn, but kept in touch until he died. When my partner passed away in 1997 he wanted me to go out there to see him, and even offered to pay for the ticket. I had a lot of problems at the time and never made it. We had lots of fun together. In fact, for a while it seemed like a non-stop party. He also helped me through some bad times. He was there for me, even when we were living so far apart. He could be critical, but in a helpful way, and always tried to make me see the funny side of a bad situation. He would be amazed that someone had written a book about him. He was a gentle man, with a lovely smile and a quick mind, and I still miss him."

Long-time friend Chris Kellett thought Jim enjoyed his life, despite the setbacks. "His outlook on life was 'That's what I want to do, and that's what I'm going to do.' He had that vision, and it came true. I think if more people had that approach the world would be a better place."

> **He didn't descend from wealthy beginnings and won his drives the old-fashioned way**

Throughout his career Jim loved being part of a team, no matter its size. Here at Brands Hatch in 1979. **Author's collection**

Sue Deakin had been by Jim's side through many of the ups and downs of his career, including accompanying him on his move stateside. "He was a very kind, thoughtful and generous person. I remember once, in Canada, he fancied a few quiet beers at the top of the CN Tower. There was a DJ there and, when we entered, he shouted through the mic, 'My God! You'll never believe who walked in here. Jimmy Crawford!' He used to receive fan letters that were just addressed 'Jim Crawford, Bolton.'"

Jim died in the internet age and news of his passing quickly spread via online motor racing forums. Although he had been out of the spotlight for several years those who had watched and admired him reacted with disbelief, as the seriousness of his health problems was not public knowledge. A selection of fan reactions:

"He had the easy smile and grace of a tough, gentle man, that great accent and was he ever fast. I remember in '92 I came in from cutting the grass, flipped on the TV and saw the speed he ran in practice. Loaded the car and drove from Atlanta to Indy early the following morning for qualifications."
Roadracer

"I've got tears in my eyes as I sit here at work typing this. I will never forget his Indy run in 1988. The crowd gave him an enormous ovation, and he obliged them – as he sat on his golf cart – by triumphantly shaking his cane in the air. RIP to one of the classiest men to race at Indy in my memory."
MichaelP

"An absolutely terrific guy and a great racer. He could do more with less than anybody I ever saw. I met him a couple of times both before and after the accident, and he never changed outwardly. May this good man rest in peace."
Oldtimer

"1980 Aurora F1 series. He did things in a F2 Chevron that defied belief. A classic example of a driver that F1 let slip away."
Mac Lark

"As mere fans we don't truly know the drivers that we watch, but Jim Crawford always seemed like a good guy. His class and wonderful sense of humor would always show through during his interviews."
TinPusher

Jim's body was flown back to the UK for cremation. A group of his closest friends then met at the Belmont Bull pub in Belmont village, a short distance from the sailing club. Jim's ashes were scattered over the water where he spent so many happy hours indulging his other great passion. Richard Jones was present at the ceremony. "I have a great affinity with Bolton, having driven for Chevron. I went to Belmont Reservoir to see Jim's ashes being scattered. I am often at the clubhouse there, and always raise a glass to Jim."

Jim was described by his close friend and sometime team manager, Bob Fernley, as "the racing driver's racing driver." It is a fitting description, for he was never a man who allowed the many fringe distractions which inevitably accompany international motor racing to detract from his focus on the main objective – beating all the other guys.

Although Jim loved driving racing cars he was by no means an avid follower of the sport. Motor racing was something he rarely watched on television, yet he did admire a select few of his contemporaries. He was thrilled to be Ronnie Peterson's team-mate during his brief foray into Formula One with Lotus. Phil Smithies also recalls an incident in 1994 when the two of them were fishing off the Florida coast. The date was May 1st and a friend on a passing boat informed them that the great Brazilian champion Ayrton Senna had died following a crash during the San Marino Grand Prix. Smithies remembers that Jim broke down in tears and was inconsolable for a few minutes before regaining his composure.

A soft spoken and gentle character, perhaps Jim was never destined for the cutthroat world of Formula One. It may well have stifled his enthusiasm for the sport he loved and the dry humour for which he was renowned. In many ways, the US lifestyle and racing scene was a much better fit.

"Coming from the racing I'd been doing, against Germans, Italians and French, there always had been a whole mix... So I feel very much a part of the scenery here. I think Americans like someone who gives their best shot, no matter where he's from."

The 500 was a race Jim became infatuated with, despite it taking so much from him. His best result of sixth in that magical 1988 race hardly does his legacy at the Speedway justice. He was one of the very best of his era. Jim himself adored the pomp and ceremony around the event. "I don't think I'll ever make a conscious decision not to come back here... I'll come back until it quits me. It's the whole atmosphere. It's pretty impressive. I'd say you could take somebody who's been dead for a couple of days, and they'd still stand up to watch the start of this race."

Ron Hemelgarn fell under the Speedway's spell and entered cars year after year. "I think I've had more than 50 cars at Indy, and finished in almost every position!" Although a rival team owner Hemelgarn was good friends with Jim. "He was a very pleasant, jovial guy. He would say things that were off the wall. We used to laugh a lot." Hemelgarn also recognised Jim's handicap at the Speedway. "He had to go on talent alone. From the mid-'80s the price of running a car would increase by one million a year. I don't think Jim was ever given the necessary equipment to show all of his talent. He could road race and he could run that speedway."

Mark Scott gives his opinion of Jim's character. "It was tough not to like Jim. He was always a very genuine person and a talented driver. I miss him as a friend and will always treasure the time we worked together. I've worked with lots of very good drivers, but cherish my friendship with Jim above all others." The 1990 500 entrant John Menard held Jim in the highest esteem. "Jim was one of the most upbeat, brave guys I've ever had the pleasure to work with. He loved speed and he was a great driver."

Kevin Hodgkinson, who had known Jim since his single-seater debut at Croft in 1972, is of a similar opinion. "He was a little bit introverted, like me. If he was speaking to a person who came from the same area that he did, he felt he was in his own comfort zone. I've always thought he was a very similar character to Bert Hawthorne. Both were very quick drivers, shy and never got the breaks they deserved. To me, Jim was an unsung hero. He was so modest with a heart of gold, even though his career had moved on and he was a force to be reckoned with in the UK. It came as no surprise when he moved over to the States, making the same impact over there. From our first meeting until the last time I saw him he never changed." Hodgkinson recounts a story which illustrates Jim's passion for the sport, and his generosity:

"A friend of mine purchased a Lotus 69 F2 car without engine, which turned out to be the car that he raced at Croft. I remember contacting Jim for help regarding the car's set-up. By this time he was driving a B29 in Formula Atlantic and making quite a name for himself. 'No problem' came the reply. 'I'll come over to Blackburn and explain it rather than tell you on the phone. I always wondered

Jim loved being on the water, and is shown here looking content on the lake at his sister Jean's house, when he returned to the UK a few months before his death. He had come to accept that his time was running out and wanted to see old friends one last time. **Boardman Family**

where that car went.' Such was his enthusiasm!"

Phil Hargreaves was with Jim at the very start of his racing adventure. "In our teenage years, several of us were amused by Jim's devil-may-care optimism. We used to imagine ourselves in old age, reminiscing, 'I knew Jim Crawford when he was a nobody, and look at him now – still a nobody.' Well, we certainly got that wrong." Joe Castellano was someone else Jim made an impression on. "He had that pleasant and smiling personality, with everyone who came into contact with him. He will be remembered as a great Scottish racer. I was so sad to hear of his death."

Renowned journalist and author Gordon Kirkby also liked what he saw. "Jim was a very good-natured guy, with a grin on his face. He was totally unpretentious, with a good heart and a keen wit."

Tom Sneva – a veteran of 21 Indianapolis 500 starts, including a race winning drive in 1983 – remembers Jim as, "a tough driver who, like a lot of other drivers, did not get the breaks to fall his way." Kenny Bernstein, the man who put his faith in Jim perhaps more than anyone, never regretted his choice. "Jim was a stand-up person, very easy going, fearless in the car and on the gas all the time. He would get everything a person could get out of the car and then some. He had a lot of guts and wasn't afraid of anything. He never made it to the top of the sport as he deserved to."

Jim's 1986 Indianapolis crew chief Roman Kuzma remembers his old driver with affection. "Jim was a great guy and a pivotal part of our racing career. We miss him immensely." Bobby Rahal admired his approach. "I first met Jim when I was doing Formula Two for Chevron, and then got to know him a bit better when he came to Indianapolis. I thought he was a super guy, and a very good driver. He wasn't a very talkative fellow. He just got on with it."

Scott Lucas – the Canadian who raced with Jim in Trinidad in 1982 – regards it as a halcyon period in his life. "Jim and Bob Howlings have both passed on, and of the four of us that went on that adventure my brother Mike and my then girlfriend Janice have died. We had the world by the tail back then. The tables have turned it seems."

The tables started turning for Jim on that fateful day at Indianapolis in 1987. It robbed a great road racer of the chance to compete on anything but ovals. Typically, Jim accepted the hand he had been given and gave all he had for the rest of his career in an effort to win the 500. He may

> He was a hoot, a great personality and a great, great human being

never have tasted the milk in Victory Lane but he lives in the memory of anyone who followed his struggles at the Speedway. Legendary Indianapolis yearbook writer Carl Hungness says of him, "Crawford was as fine a competitor as I have ever met."

Willy T Ribbs remembers his old friend very fondly. "I first met Jim at a party at Indy. He was fun to party with. There was nothing boring about Crawford! I couldn't compete with him drinking. Even Bobby Unser didn't want to drink with Crawford! He was a hoot, a great personality and a great, great human being. There are a lot of people who live until 95 and don't do five percent of what Jim did."

Keith Leighton always enjoyed being in Jim's company, professionally or socially. "A quiet evening meal with Jim was never going to happen! No matter how bad or good the day's events were, Jim would have his take on them. Once he started, the laughter ensued to the point where your belly ached – a glorious feeling that I sorely miss. His repertoire of jokes was some of the best you could hear, especially when spoken in that dry accent of his. Jim was a true character that all of Scotland should be proud to have had as one of their ambassadors."

Fellow racer Tommy Byrne rated Jim highly. "He was a gentleman, a great guy. But most importantly he could drive the shit out of every car that he got into. He was one of the good guys in racing and is sorely missed." Bob Abdellah had dealings with Jim out of the cockpit, working in public relations. "I had the pleasure of working with Jim during his IMSA Camel GT and Indycar racing days. I can think of few more lion-hearted drivers in his day. Generally quiet and under-spoken, he had an agile mind and a wry, dry understated wit."

The final words are from David Hutson, without whose cajoling this book would not exist. "I found my friend Jim to be a kind and gentle man, a tremendous, fast and brave racer. In his years in the US he impressed many people: racers, team owners, journalists and the general racing public who grew to become great fans."

It is impossible to say what Jim may have achieved had the cards fallen differently for him. His natural shyness and inability to embrace the commercial side of the sport certainly hampered his career. Perhaps with a brasher attitude and willingness to talk up his own abilities he may have achieved even more, but then he wouldn't have been the Jim Crawford so universally loved. In motor racing, his type are a rare breed.

Index

A

Abdellah, Bob 98, 127
Adcox, Gerald 118
Aintree 23, 25
Alexis 21-23
AMCO 61, 71
Andretti, Mario 75-76, 85, 99, 111-112
Andretti, Michael 76, 81, 83, 86-87
Arnold, Susan 95
Ashmore, Bruce 99, 103, 111, 115
Ashton, Tom 17, 21, 23
Atkinson, Paddy 35, 43, 87, 103
Axford, Jeff 18

B

Bailey, Neil
Belli, Tino 79, 86
Belmont 16, 44, 46, 103, 123, 126
Bennett, Derek 23, 36, 39, 43-44, 46
Bergandi, Hector Luis 93
Bernstein, Kenny 10, 89-92, 95, 98-99, 103, 107, 112-113, 127
Bettenhausen, Gary 100, 111, 121, 123
Boardman, Charles 17
Boardman, Jean 15-16, 18

Bolton 12, 15-17, 19, 23, 25, 28, 32, 43-44, 46, 57, 70, 121, 123, 125-126
Bond, Bev 32
Booth, Warren 52, 54
Brabham 62-63
Brands Hatch 25-27, 29-31, 36, 38, 41, 43-44, 50-52, 60-61
Bridges, John 23, 25
Brise, Tony 28, 30-31, 36-41
Buick 10, 81-83, 85, 89, 91, 93, 96-97, 100-101, 103-105, 107-111, 121
Byrne, Tommy 70, 127

C

Caesars Palace 66
Carr, Paul 23, 41
Castellano, Giuseppe 'Joe' 60-61, 65, 127
Catt, Ian 41
Chandhok, Vicky 71, 73
Chapman, Colin 35, 37, 40-41
Chapman, David 122-123
Chevrolet 115
Chevron 23, 25-29, 31, 33, 36, 38-40, 43-47, 49, 51-52, 54-55, 57-60, 69-71, 73, 125-126
Choularton, Charlie 21
Choularton, Steve 21-23,

25, 28, 30-32, 35-37, 124
Clark, Jim 11, 13, 35, 76, 90
Connel, John 51-52, 65, 67, 125
Conte Racing 82-83
Cook, Derek 38
Cort, Richard 16, 19, 47
Crawford, Alexander 15, 17-18, 32
Crawford, Annie (mother) 15-16, 18, 32
Crawford, Annie (wife) 121-124
Crawford, Emily 115, 122
Crawford, Jeffrey 93, 103
Crawford, Jean 15-16, 18
Crawford, Jim throughout
Crawford, Sheila 83, 86-87, 91, 93, 103-104, 115, 121
Croft 22-23, 59-60
Crompton, Rod 21
Crosby, Rick 67

D

Daly, Derek 85-86, 112, 115, 118, 121
Davidson, Donald 75-76, 92
Davies, Phil 16, 124
Deakin, Sue 17, 66, 125
Dean, Tony 22-23
Dent, Stuart 59
Depailler, Patrick 37
Devaney, Bernard 62-63

Dodson, Rodney 50, 61
Donington Park 49-50, 60-61, 70
Donnison, Janet 17, 33, 61, 89, 123-124
Dron, Tony 45
Dunfermline 15, 52, 104
Dunnell, Paul 71

E

Edwards, Neil 23, 25
Elkhart Lake 69
Ensign 60-61, 65-69, 71, 107

F

Fernley, Bob 60-62, 65-67, 69-71, 73, 75, 124, 126
Fittipaldi, Emerson 91, 95, 104, 113, 115
Foyt, AJ 81, 112
Free, David 69
Frey, Walter 44
Friswell, Geoff 29, 31, 38

G

Ganz, Whitney 82-83, 124
Gill, Dave 47, 89
Glasgow 15
Glass, Arnold 60, 69
Gonsalves, Gordon 63
Good, Brian 67, 93
Goodliff, Geoff 28
Goodwood 29, 36

Graham, John 66-67, 70
Green Valley Raceway 71
Griffiths, Tony 28
Grovewood Award 32-33
Guerrero, Roberto 107, 111-113, 115

H
Hagenbauer, Henning 61
Hargreaves, Phil 17, 127
Hemelgarn, Ron 87, 118, 126
Henton, Brian 39-40
Herd, Robin 29, 78
Hockenheim 57
Hodgkinson, Kevin 23, 29, 43, 126
Howlings, Bob 21, 23, 61-62, 127
Humphreys, Keith 23
Hungness, Carl 127
Hutson, David 12, 79, 81, 86, 92, 127

I
Ickx, Jacky 39
Indianapolis 10-13, 35, 75-78, 80, 85-87, 89-91, 93, 95, 100-101, 103, 107, 112, 116, 121, 126-127
Ingliston 49-50
Isis School 16

J
Jeffrey, Andrew 49
Jones, Alan 29-31, 37
Jones, Richard 21-22, 43, 124, 126

K
Karlskoga 47
Kellett, Chris 43-44, 59, 124
Kennedy, David 70
Kessler, Freddy 44
Kirby, Gordon 93, 111, 127
Knutstorp 47
Kuzma, Roman 13, 78-79, 81, 87, 124, 127

L
Laguna Seca 66, 77
Lawlor, Alo 49-50
Lee, Rod 16-17, 21-22, 124
Leighton, Keith 37, 78, 81, 127

Leslie, David 62
Lime Rock 67
Little Colonsay 15
Lodge, Mark 93
Lola 12, 73, 77-78, 89, 91, 93, 95-101, 103-105, 107-111, 115-116, 121
Long Beach 75-76, 78, 80
Lotus 22-23, 30, 35-41, 50, 78, 124
Lucas, Scott 62-63, 127

M
Madras 71, 73
Mallock, Ray 31, 49-50
Mallory Park 28-31, 36, 39-41, 43, 45, 47, 49-52
Mallya, Vijay 71, 73
Manchester 21, 32
Marcelo, Jovy 113
March 10, 22-23, 28-31, 69- 70, 77-79, 81-83, 85-86
Mather, Kim 51-52, 54
May, Nick 41
Meadowlands 77-78
Mears, Rick 10, 12, 76, 79, 81, 86-87, 91-92, 95, 111, 113
Menard, John 100, 113, 118, 123, 126
Methodist Hospital 10, 86, 101, 111, 113
Miller, Robin 122
Mini 16-17, 19
Misano 59
Mondello Park 30, 32, 49
Monza 41, 52
Moores, Rob 45, 47, 61, 123
Morgan, Dave 29-31, 39
Morgan, Richard 36-37, 39
Mosley, Max 29
Mosport 66, 69, 71
Mugello 57
Muir, Bob 41

N
Newman, Paul 92
Nicholson, John 25, 28- 31
Nilsson, Gunnar 41
Nogaro 30, 40
Nürburgring 45, 57

O
Ongais, Danny 79
Opert, Fred 31, 33, 36

Oulton Park 25, 28-29, 31, 39, 43, 45-47, 50, 52, 54-55, 60-62, 66, 69-70

P
Paisley 15
Patrick, Pat 85
Pau 57-58
Paul Ricard 22, 38, 47, 49
Parker, 'Fess' 21
Peers, Mike 12, 25, 35, 44-47, 49, 51, 54, 60, 65, 79, 82, 90, 123, 125
Peterson, Ronnie 30, 36-41, 126
Phoenix International Raceway 98, 100
Phoenix Park 30
Plygrange 49, 51-52, 54-55, 57-60
Purley, David 25, 31
Pye, Marcus 52

R
Rahal, Bobby 81, 101, 115, 127
Rainford, John 21
Ralt 69
Reynard 118
Ribbs, Willy T 104, 111, 115-116, 127
Richardson, Geoff 41
Riley, Bob 116
Rising-Moore, Rick 13, 124
Riverside 65-66
Road Atlanta 71
Robinson, Brian 51
Roe, Michael 70
Rosyth 15
Roux, George 103, 121, 123

S
Sailing 16, 103
Scott, Mark 10, 86-87, 89, 92, 95, 111, 116, 118, 121, 123, 126
Scott, Richard 28
Sears Point 69-70
Shuttleworth, Jeff 15, 18, 118
Silverstone 28-29, 36-41, 46, 50-53, 57, 60-62, 75
Smith, Paul 50

Smithies, Phil 37, 121, 124, 126
Snetterton 25, 31, 36, 39, 50, 52
Sneva, Tom 75, 80, 113, 127
Spa-Francorchamps 57, 59
Sproston, Richard 16, 43
Stiller, Harry 32
Sullivan, Danny 79, 81, 90, 95
Surtees 29, 35
Switzerland 12, 44-46, 49

T
Taylor, Dave 41, 43, 46
Team Harper 29-31, 40
Thatcher, Mark 60
Theodore 75-77, 107
Thruxton 31, 33, 43, 46, 52, 57, 60
Toleman 57, 59
Trammell, Dr. Terry 10, 86
Trois Rivières 66-67, 69, 70
Tyrrell, Ken 35

U
Unser, Al 112, 115
Unser, Bobby 91, 127

V
Vallelunga 47, 57
Vandervell, Colin 37
Villeneuve, Jacques 66-67, 69-70, 77

W
Wachs, Eddie 75
Wallerfield 61-62
Watkins Glen, 82-83
Wentz, Ted 29-31, 37, 40, 124
Werran, Geoff 44
Wheldon, Dan 122-123
Williams, Barrie 51, 70
Williams, Cyd 28-29
Winkelhock, Manfred 52-53
Wood, Geoff 36, 38
Wysard 77-79

Z
Zandvoort 45

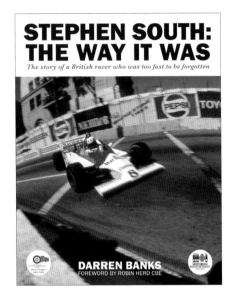

Stephen South: The Way it Was
Darren Banks

Stephen South was a young British racing driver in the '70s who looked set for the glory that ultimately fell to Nigel Mansell. One went on to become one of the nation's most loved characters, the other's career faded in the cruel circumstances.

This is a multi-faceted tale of struggle, success, disappointment, controversy, the continuous battle for funding and recognition and, ultimately, heartbreak.

RAC Motoring Book of the Year finalist and Michael Sedgwick Award finalist.
ISBN 978-0-9576450-2-8

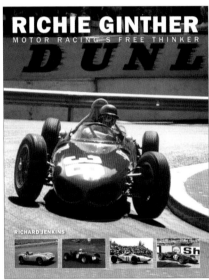

Richie Ginther: Motor Racing's Free Thinker
Richard Jenkins

For many years it was believed that Richie Ginther, one of Formula One's best-known drivers of the 1960s, later became an angry, reclusive bum; a hero-to-zero tale. The first ever authorised biography of Ginther reveals that he enjoyed astonishing triumphs and led an enriched life after leaving motorsport. Meticulously researched and packed with memories from family, friends and fellow racers.

RAC Motoring Book of the Year winner and Montagu of Beaulieu Trophy winner.
ISBN 978-0-9576450-5-9

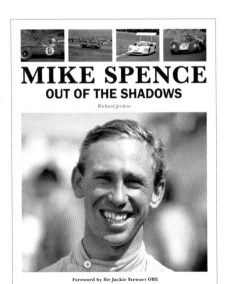

Mike Spence: Out of the Shadows
Richard Jenkins

Mike Spence was one of the most likeable and respected grand prix drivers of the 1960s and forged a reputation as an outstanding development driver. He was at his peak and on the cusp of winning the Indianapolis 500 when he was killed in a practice accident at the Indianapolis Motor Speedway in 1968.

This is the definitive and only authorised biography of his life and has all the hallmarks that made author Richard Jenkins' first book, *Richie Ginther: Motor Racing's Free Thinker*, a double award winner.
ISBN 978-0-9576450-9-7

Gerry Birrell: Lost Before His Time
Darren Banks

Up-and-coming Scottish ace Gerry Birrell was on the verge of achieving his ambition to reach the pinnacle of motorsport when he needlessly lost his life at the Rouen-Les-Essarts circuit.

After moving south, he climbed the motorsport ranks and became a Ford Motor Company works driver. Opinions vary on whether he would have been a success in Formula One had the rumoured drive for Tyrrell become a reality.

This is a comprehensive, detailed account of a versatile career of an often overlooked and forgotten racer of immense promise.
ISBN 978-1-7391249-1-5

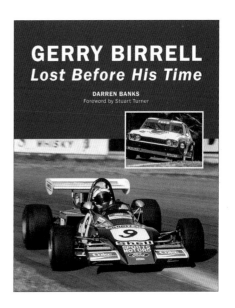

Tom Pryce: Memories of a Welsh F1 Star
Darren Banks and Kevin Guthrie

Tom Pryce, the self-effacing driver from rural Wales, lit up grand prix racing in the 1970s. More than four decades on from his untimely death in the 1977 South African Grand Prix, those who knew him share their memories in this unique and touching tribute.
ISBN 978-0-9576450-7-3

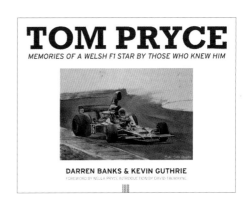

Is There Much More of This?
Andrew Marriott

Veteran motorsport journalist Andrew Marriott writes with a light and humorous touch about a multi-faceted career covering some six decades. He has been driven across Buenos Aires by Juan Manuel Fangio, starred in a hilarious TV blooper episode with Mario Andretti, judged competitions with James Hunt and offered a flat floor for Jody Scheckter to sleep on.

There is plenty to draw upon for this enjoyable collection of tales of tracks, travels and TV from a life and career lived at the very heart of motorsport.
ISBN 978-1-7391249-0-8

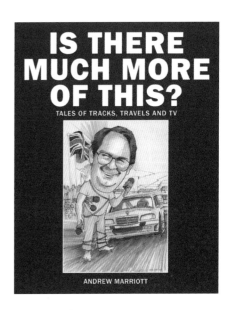

Selected Bibliography

The British at Indianapolis (Wagstaff, 2010)
Indianapolis 500 Yearbooks (Hungness) 1984 to 1995
1992 Pittsburgh Vintage Grand Prix Programme
Autosport
Motoring News
Motor Sport
RK News Brief
Arizona Republic
Bolton Chronicle
Bolton Evening News
Chicago Tribune
The Des Moines Register
Detroit Free Press
Fort Worth Star-Telegram
The Glasgow Herald
The Independent
The Indianapolis News
Indianapolis Star
Indy Star
The Kansas City Star
LA Times
Leader-Telegram
The Miami Herald
New York Times
Pensacola News Journal
Sun Sentinel
Tampa Bay Times

As he will be remembered, laughing and smiling. Throughout a career which brought much disappointment and physical pain, in addition to the many high points, Jim faced any adversity which came his way with good humour and steely resolve. **Alejandro de Brito.**

About the Author

This is Kevin's second book for Performance Publishing, following the release of Tom Pryce, Memories Of a Welsh F1 Star by Those Who Knew Him, written in collaboration with close friend, Darren Banks. Kevin has been a racing fan for over 30 years, and grew up just a few miles from the Knockhill circuit in Scotland. Outside of racing he is a professional musician and co-founder of an award-winning music education company. A keen historian in his spare time, he has self-published two local history books. Kevin lives with his partner and two children in Fife, Scotland.